SUPER BOWL HEROES

SUPER BOWL HEROES

BARRY WILNER & KEN RAPPOPORT

Guilford, Connecticut

An imprint of Rowman & Littlefield

Distributed by NATIONAL BOOK NETWORK

Copyright © 2016 by Barry Wilner & Ken Rappoport

British Library Cataloguing in Publication Information Available

Library of Congress Cataloging-in-Publication Data

Names: Wilner, Barry, author. | Rappoport, Ken, author.
Title: Super Bowl heroes / Barry Wilner & Ken Rappoport.
Description: Guilford, Connecticut : Lyons Press, an imprint of Rowman & Littlefield, [2016]
Identifiers: LCCN 2016016349 (print) | LCCN 2016018565 (ebook) | ISBN 9781493018758 (pbk. : alk. paper) | ISBN 9781493018765 (e-book)
Subjects: LCSH: Super Bowl—History. | Football players—Biography. | Football—United States—History.
Classification: LCC GV956.2.S8 W554 2016 (print) | LCC GV956.2.S8 (ebook) | DDC 796.332/64809—dc23
LC record available at https://lccn.loc.gov/2016016349

♾™ The paper used in this publication meets the minimum requirements of American National Standard for Information Sciences—Permanence of Paper for Printed Library Materials, ANSI/NISO Z39.48-1992.

For Larry, Becka, and Maddie: What a team!
–Ken

To Helene, the best there has ever been. Stay strong.
–Barry

Contents

ACKNOWLEDGMENTS

NANCY ARMOUR, GEORGE ATALLAH, HOWARD BALZER, JUDY BATTISTA, Gil Brandt, Joe Browne, Simmi Buttar, Rachel Cohen, Steve Cohen, Jim Corbett, Tim Dahlberg, Bob Glauber, Joanna Hunter, Pat Kirwan, Alex Marvez, Brian McCarthy, Robbie Mendelson, Jim Miller, Paul Montella, Nick Pavlatos, Bill Polian, Frank Ramos, Jilane Rodgers, Adam Schein, Michael Signora, and Jim Steeg

INTRODUCTION

FOR HALF A CENTURY THE SUPER BOWL HAS BEEN CONSIDERED THE prime sports event of the NFL, topping off the season with hoopla, hyperbole, halftime extravaganzas, and, yes, even a football game that crowns a champion.

It has become akin to a national holiday—just check out the number of sick days at businesses throughout America on the Monday following the big game.

Now after reaching its 50th anniversary, it is a perfect time to look back at the game.

Did you know it wasn't always called the Super Bowl? The first two editions were called simply the "AFL-NFL championship game."

So how did it get its everlasting name? Read on: Super Bowl I through Super Bowl 50 are ready for kickoff in this book.

Each of the game's MVPs are profiled in Super Bowl Heroes with stories of the football players at their best in the biggest game. The long line of Super Bowl MVPs stretches from the 1960s, when Green Bay's Bart Starr won the award twice, to Denver's Von Miller in 2016, Super Bowl 50.

Along with the MVP winners, the book discusses such outstanding performances in the ultimate game as Timmy Smith's sensational and surprising rushing performance in Super Bowl XXII and David Tyree's amazing catch against his helmet in Super Bowl XLII.

And don't forget the coaches: Profiled are Super Bowl Coaching Heroes, and Super Bowl Antihero coaches.

We even take a look at the villains of Super Bowl lore.

Leading off with Doug Williams, the first African-American MVP quarterback, Super Bowl Heroes will thrill, delight and educate all football fans.

First down, ready to go.

DOUG WILLIAMS

It seems absurd nowadays that a big deal ever was made about African-American quarterbacks in the NFL. Back in 1988, it was an overriding theme for the Super Bowl.

And when the hero of that game in San Diego was, indeed, a black QB, Doug Williams, the racial overtones of the Redskins vs. Broncos in Super Bowl XXII were exacerbated.

Then they pretty much disappeared.

Today, with Russell Wilson having guided Seattle to two straight NFL title games, and with Donovan McNabb, Steve McNair, and Colin Kaepernick leading their teams into various Super Bowls, race isn't an issue. Nor should it ever have been. Indeed, there were a dozen black quarterbacks in the NFL when Wilson faced off with Tom Brady in Super Bowl XLIX. Yet Williams vs. John Elway was billed by many as being very much about the color of each player's skin. "Nobody said the Washington Redskins against the Denver Broncos, which is what it really was," Williams said years later. "It was me, a black quarterback, against the great John Elway" (who happened to be white, dubbed by some as "The Golden Boy"). So it was predictable and understandable when Washington's victory and Williams's MVP performance were considered groundbreaking.

"I visualized me being in his shoes, and it's a reality now," McNabb said before the 2005 Super Bowl in which his Eagles played New England. "I'm just looking forward to the challenge of getting on that football field. If I can do some of the things he did in that particular game, I'll be excited as well."

McNair, who like Williams was from the Deep South and, like Williams, was a victim of racial prejudice during his childhood, called Williams "a player who meant everything to us."

"What we as black kids and black football players could take from that Super Bowl was a sense of sharing with Doug Williams what he had achieved," McNair once said. "It's impossible to measure how inspiring that was."

Not hard for the Reverend Jesse Jackson to gauge it, though: "This is one of the great moments in American history. It comes 60 years after Jackie Robinson broke through. It's an American feel-good moment."

Here's how good Williams was on the last day of January 1988: After Washington fell behind 10–0 in the first quarter, it put together the best 15-minute span in Super Bowl history. The Redskins scored 35 unanswered points, with Williams connecting on four touchdown throws. In one period. In all, Williams passed for 340 yards and oversaw an offense that gained 602, with unheralded running back Timmy Smith going for a record 204.

That Doug Williams made the breakthrough was against most odds, given his checkered performances in the NFL.

A brilliant passer at Grambling State, a predominantly black school in Louisiana, Williams was selected only 17th in the 1978 draft because, well, he went to a predominantly black school in Louisiana. The "wisdom" of the day was that African-American quarterbacks would be fine in the NFL—if they changed positions. Consider that in the same draft, Washington's Warren Moon, a mobile passer and runner and crafty creator, was not drafted at all. Moon had to head to Canada to begin his professional career. (Of course, Moon would make it back to the NFL and now has a bust in the Hall of Fame.)

Williams was tall (6'4"), well built, and had a rocket arm. He wound up being the only quarterback in that entire draft who made any true impact in the NFL.

But it took time. And with each struggle he experienced during four and a half seasons as a starter in Tampa—forget his two seasons in the USFL—then in one season as a backup to Jay Schroeder in Washington, when he often ran the scout team, the louder the ludicrous chorus grew about black QBs not having the skills to be a champion. Indeed, Williams complained in Tampa that Bucs fans and even team management would have treated a white quarterback differently.

Late in the 1987 season finale, Williams replaced a struggling Schroeder and led the Redskins to an overtime win. That left coach

Joe Gibbs with a tough decision for the postseason opener at Chicago: Schroeder or Williams?

Williams was 0-2 as a starter, 3-0 as a sub. Gibbs gambled that the guy who had come off the bench was the right guy for the playoffs.

"You see those year-end lists of who's in and who's out, and I've been in and out most of 1987," Williams told The Associated Press. "Luckily, I go into 1988 as in."

Two games later, with victories over Chicago and Minnesota again, he had the Redskins in the Super Bowl.

Super Bowl XXII's Media Day was not the first circus of the eccentric, not with the Raiders and Bears having made recent appearances in the big game. It was, however, distressingly bizarre, particularly when this Q and A took place, according to the AP:

Williams was asked either "Doug, obviously you've been a black quarterback all your life. When did race begin to matter to people?" or "How long have you been a black quarterback?" Some reported that Williams misheard the first question and thought he was asked the second. Williams always has said he actually was asked how long he'd been a black quarterback.

Legend has Williams answering: "I've been black all my life, been a quarterback since I was a kid."

In reality . . .

"The way I answered it was the fact that I had been a black quarterback only when I left Grambling," he said. "Because when I left Grambling, I was just Grambling's quarterback."

And after that?

"Every article that was written, every adjective was 'Tampa's black quarterback' or 'black quarterback Doug Williams,'" he said. "It was never just the way it is today."

Who is behind center today throughout the NFL is judged almost entirely by talent. Race no longer matters.

Thank Doug Williams for that.

THE 1960s

Super Bowl I, II

Before the Super Bowl got its name, there was the Ice Bowl. BRRRRR!!!!!

It was December 31, 1967. And there was Bart Starr, cooler than ever on one of the coldest New Year's Eves, even by Green Bay standards. The temperature was 13 below zero with a brisk 15-mile-per-hour wind. The Packers were playing the Dallas Cowboys for the National Football League championship. Winner goes to the second AFL-NFL Championship Game, loser goes home—frozen. Green Bay had beaten Dallas the previous season in the NFL title game to go to the first Super Bowl, even though the ultimate pro football championship contest did not have that name yet.

Starr had taken a rough road to get to this point. He had more downs than ups in his early career. Because he was so polite and introverted, coaches chose other, more aggressive players. In high school, it was only when the starting quarterback broke his leg that the coach was forced to turn to Starr. He led them to their first undefeated season.

Winning all-state and All-America honors, Starr chose to attend Alabama to be near his girlfriend. He saw little action, so to get on the field, he became the team's punter with a 41.4-yard average, second best in the nation. But he sprained his back in his junior year and was benched in his senior year while the coach tried out younger players, and the NFL seemed to be an impossible dream.

Alabama's basketball coach had different ideas. He contacted a personal friend, the personnel director of the Packers, praising Starr. Even though he only played briefly for the Crimson Tide, Starr's stats were impressive. He was picked in the 1956 draft 199th overall—oddly, the same spot that another Super Bowl hero, Tom Brady, would be chosen 43 years later.

Once again, Starr was on the sidelines in his rookie year with the Packers. Indeed, in 1956, 1957, and 1958, he had few chances to play and the Packers suffered three straight losing seasons. In '58, they finished 1-10-1.

Starr was uncomfortable with coach Scooter McLean's lack of rules and play selection. Players missed meetings, set their own dress codes, and didn't worry about curfews. Actually, there weren't any.

Then McLean was out, Vince Lombardi was in. And once again, Starr was overlooked. "He was probably just a little too polite, and maybe just a little too self-effacing, to be the real, tough, bold quarterback [you] must be in the National Football League," Lombardi said at the time.

Starr was relegated to holding the ball on kicks while Lamar McHan and Joe Francis rotated at quarterback. When McHan was injured and Green Bay went on a five-game losing streak, Starr got his break. He led the Packers on a five-game winning streak that gave them a winning record for the first time in 12 years.

The job was Starr's, but Lombardi was not easy to play for, even when the team was winning. And he was especially hard on Starr, screaming at him in front of the whole team for any error. Starr took it for a while, since he had been brought up in a military family. He knew all about discipline and following orders. But soon enough was enough.

One day, he marched into Lombardi's office and responded in full. After that day, there were no more public beratings and Lombardi had his championship-quality quarterback.

"Starr impressed me from the beginning the way he went about getting himself ready for the game," Lombardi said. "I was impressed by his memory. I was impressed by his dedication."

Starr grew to love playing for Lombardi, a strict disciplinarian. Starr, under Lombardi, became one of the game's greatest clutch performers. He was more than ready to, well, star in the 1967 NFL title game against Dallas, soon to be known as the Ice Bowl.

The Packers scored the first time they got the ball, and then scored in the second quarter to take a 14–0 lead over the Cowboys. Cowboys quarterback Don Meredith was having trouble with the cold. "My hand grew colder with each drive," Meredith said, who was missing his receivers. Nevertheless, the Cowboys rallied to cut Green Bay's lead to 14–10 at the half.

Meredith cut a hole in his jersey and tucked his hand inside to keep his passing hand warm between plays. It worked.

The Cowboys started to dominate in the second half. They led for the first time, 17–14. In the fourth period, with 4:50 to go, the Packers had possession on their 31. Starr was faced with the monumental task of moving his team nearly 70 yards down a field that had become a slippery, icy pond.

Green Bay's chances remained remote at this point.

Facing Dallas's "Doomsday Defense," Starr moved the Packers to the Cowboys 1 yard line. Starr called for two running plays for Donny Anderson, who was stopped for no gain. "He almost fell down before I could get the ball to him the second time he carried," Starr said. "I knew Donnie wasn't getting any footing."

Starr called a timeout to talk things over with Lombardi. The quarterback told the coach that he wanted to run a "31 wedge," an inside running play where he follows Jerry Kramer's blocking over the goal line. "Run it," Lombardi said, "and let's get the hell out of here."

On third down and goal to go, that's just what Starr did. With Kramer leading the way, Starr squeezed into the end zone to give the Packers a 21–17 victory.

Next stop: Miami, to play the Oakland Raiders for the second "world championship."

The previous year, the first event matching the top teams from the National Football League and American Football League, pitted Lombardi's Packers against the Kansas City Chiefs. It began a new era in professional football following a heated power struggle between the two leagues that ended with their merger. And the Super Bowl game was an essential step toward unification between the two leagues—no merger agreement could have been done without it.

At the time, not many fans of the established league knew much about the AFL, which was generally regarded as a second-tier league in comparison. The AFL champion Kansas City Chiefs were two-touchdown underdogs to the Packers, which Chiefs fullback Curtis McClinton thought was ridiculous. McClinton thought the Packers should have been favored by three points at best, and only because "they have a strong big-game history."

Packers defensive end Willie Davis summed it up succinctly: "It was not a game we were playing for the Packers, but for the NFL itself, for a way of life, a game of survival, a test of manhood."

The Packers' dynasty was on the line: Green Bay virtually dominated the league from 1961 through 1967. In the week before the game, Lombardi put his team through grueling and intense practices. "We were all wondering, what the hell was Vince doing?" said Bob Skoronski, the Packers left tackle and co-captain. "It was one of the few times in my career I was afraid that we might leave the game on the practice field."

The Chiefs outweighed the Packers by 15 pounds per man, on both sides. They were a young team. "Great talent, bad habits," Packers linebacker Dave Robinson said, "but they were so much better than the rest of the AFL that they could get away with it."

The Packers were 13½-point favorites on game day. Tickets were priced at $12, $10, and $6. More than 31,000 seats were unsold at the Los Angeles Coliseum.

It was a warm, windless day. Temperatures were in the 70s. Starr waited a while before opening up his offense. Max McGee caught the first touchdown pass from Starr, a circus catch that went for 37 yards. "It was one of the finest catches I've ever seen, because I was hit as I threw the ball, and most of the zip was taken off it," Starr told the *Palm Beach Post*. "He reached two feet behind him, and pulled it in and went for the score."

Another touchdown pass by Starr was nullified by a penalty, leaving the Packers holding a slim 14–10 lead at the half. Although they were in the lead, the Packers were hardly dominating the game.

"At halftime I felt pretty darn good," said Chiefs owner Lamar Hunt. "We had more yards and more first downs than the Packers and we were moving the ball on them."

In the Packers locker room, Lombardi was telling his players to relax, they were too tight. "Well, he was the guy who'd gotten us so nervous in the first place," said middle linebacker Ray Nitschke. The Packers relaxed and pulled away in the second half and won 35–10.

Starr was especially successful on third-down conversions, completing 10 of 13. Overall he completed 16 of 23 passes for 250 yards.

Starr received the first MVP award, and shared in the winner's purse of $15,000 a man. The losers each received $7,500.

So the Packers were old hands at this when they went up against the Raiders in Miami—a game that featured more heroics by Starr, with a little help from his friends.

One of those friends was Boyd Dowler, who caught a 62-yard touchdown pass from Starr. The Packers quarterback found Dowler wide open deep in the middle of the field and the receiver raced 62 yards for a TD and a 13–0 Green Bay lead.

"I just bulled by Kent McCloughan," Dowler told *Sports Illustrated*. "He was playing me tight and he bumped me and I ran right through him. It was a little post pattern, and when I got by no one was left."

It was part of the 202 yards collected by Starr, who completed 13 of 24 passes. "They killed us," Raiders defensive tackle Tom Keating told the *Boston Globe*. Yes, but it wasn't until Starr connected with McGee in the third quarter on a key 35-yard play that the Raiders were truly dead.

It was third down and inches on the Green Bay 40 with the Packers leading 16–7. Starr faked a fullback plunge into the line, then backpedaled and lofted a pass to McGee, who had replaced Dowler. It was a play the Packers used successfully time and again throughout the season, but it seemed like a complete surprise to the Raiders.

"One of the safeties woke up late," McGee said. "He started over and Bart saw him and adjusted to throw away from him."

McGee turned around to catch the ball. "It was a great throw by Bart," McGee said.

The play set up Donny Anderson's touchdown that sealed the Raiders' downfall.

Final: Green Bay 33, Oakland 14.

Once again, Starr won the Super Bowl MVP award as the Lombardi era came to a close in Green Bay. With the victory, Starr became the only NFL quarterback to lead a team to three straight championships, a record that still stands. He also stands alone with five NFL titles, including the first two Super Bowls.

McGee, Lombardi, and the First Super Bowl

Curfew time. Do you know where your football players are? Particularly Max McGee, veteran receiver of the Green Bay Packers.

Coach Vince Lombardi had his hands full trying to keep tabs on his errant pass catcher. McGee had been fined regularly for breaking curfew.

You have to understand McGee. He was a happy-go-lucky guy who loved to entertain his teammates and keep things light in the locker room. So you could understand coming off a week of practice hell under Lombardi before Super Bowl I that McGee wanted to cut loose that evening.

But there was a formidable obstacle.

"When we got to L.A. on Saturday, I just had to hit the streets," McGee said, "but Vince had set a $10,000 fine if you broke curfew."

McGee didn't expect to play in the game. He had seen little action during the season, catching only four passes. So he invited Paul Hornung to go help him paint the town. Hornung was suffering from an injury and didn't expect to play, either. They had met a couple of stewardesses, but had to get back to the hotel for bed check.

"I stayed dressed and just got under the covers and waited to be marked down as present," said McGee. "Paul was worried about the fine." McGee went out, had a great time; Hornung stayed in.

"I got back to the room between 7:30 and 8:00 to get Hornung up for breakfast," McGee said with a chuckle. "That was one of my jobs; that's why Lombardi kept me around an extra two years."

But there was no kidding around for McGee when it came to watching game films. On more than one occasion, Lombardi was showing films when McGee would utter something quietly.

"What did you say?" Lombardi asked as he stopped the projector. Lombardi reran the play as McGee made his observation known; Lombardi valued McGee's insight. Even though he didn't expect to play, McGee had paid attention when the Chiefs' game films were shown.

Now it was game time. McGee and Hornung sat on the bench, just relaxing, talking about Paul's wedding plans. Paul asked his friend, "What would you do if you had to play?" McGee answered, "I'd be surprised."

What happened next belonged in a Hollywood movie. Boyd Dowler, the Packers' No. 1 receiver, reinjured his shoulder and was forced to leave the game shortly after kickoff.

McGee suddenly heard Lombardi calling his name. Uh oh, McGee thought, somehow Lombardi had found out about him breaking curfew and decided to fine him then and there.

No such luck. He was actually going to play, hangover and all. "I couldn't find my helmet, so I borrowed one from a lineman," McGee said.

Starr called a pass play for McGee. The quarterback was hit just as he released the pass. The ball sailed off course, two feet behind McGee.

"Let's face it, it was a rotten pass," McGee said. "You pay a guy $100,000 to throw to a $25,000 end, you expect him to throw better than that. I wasn't going to go back and get killed by some linebacker.

"I thought sure somebody was going to intercept the ball. So I reached back to knock it down, to break up the interception, and when I did, the ball stuck in my hand. Just like that. Stuck right in my hand."

He had just completed a 37-yard touchdown play, the first points scored in Super Bowl history.

McGee caught six more passes, including another for a TD, for a total of 138 yards. The Packers won easily, 35–10. With seven receptions and two TDs, McGee made the cover of *Sports Illustrated*. He retired from football after winning a second Super Bowl the next year and wore his championship rings proudly—one of the most unlikely of Super Bowl heroes.

Super Bowl III

NEVER MIND THAT THE NATIONAL FOOTBALL LEAGUE'S RECORD BOOK shows the first Super Bowl was played in 1967. It was actually 1969.

Oh, sure, there was a league championship game in 1967 when the NFL's Green Bay Packers beat the American Football League's Kansas City Chiefs. And another in 1968, when the Packers defeated the AFL's Oakland Raiders. But the hyperbolic title first appeared on a program cover in 1969 for the Jets-Colts battle, the first official Super Bowl.

The first two games were relative warmups when compared to the one played in 1969 when Joe Namath made his famous (infamous in Baltimore) guarantee and changed the face of football.

The pressure was on Namath's New York Jets. Big time. Since the NFL had merged with the AFL in 1966 after a long and bitter battle, an expected pattern was developing, with NFL teams dominating the title game. Another loss by an AFL team in the so-called "World Championship Game" and there would be serious doubts about the AFL's right to be on the same field with the NFL. Even a close game, which was not expected, would prove the merger valid.

The Jets were overwhelming underdogs to the Baltimore Colts, an NFL powerhouse that had lost only one game all season in what was generally considered the stronger league. The betting line in Las Vegas: a ridiculous 19 points. "Our pride was hurt a little bit because of the odds they were giving," Namath said.

But the Colts were recognized as one of pro football's greatest teams. A team of hardened veterans, the Colts had handily whipped the Cleveland Browns 34–0 in the NFL title game. The Jets had defeated the Oakland Raiders 27–23 in the AFL title game.

Then came the guarantee.

On January 9, 1969, three days before the game, Namath was invited to the Miami Touchdown Club luncheon to be honored as the Pro Football Player of the Year. He wasn't sure he wanted to go. "I was just hoping for a quiet night back at the hotel, but it was an important honor, so I went," Namath said. "I knew going to south Miami, though, things could get kind of wild." They did, but not for the reason that Namath thought.

The quarterback was commonly known as "Broadway Joe" because of his flamboyant lifestyle. He was making more money than anyone in football thanks to a record-setting $400,000 contract he signed with the Jets. The huge contract helped to settle the football war between the AFL and NFL. Owners on both sides were fearful that the spending for players would spiral out of control unless the leagues came together on a merger deal.

While in New York, Namath led the league in partying. A magnet for women, no player was more stylish. Namath could often be seen in a white fur coat with a beautiful girl (and sometimes two) on his arm.

Namath was the face of football when it came to endorsing products. Doing sexy spots with an unknown model, Farrah Fawcett, Namath hawked shaving cream. He also stripped down to do underwear ads for Jockey. And he pitched Right Guard deodorant.

But it was an endorsement deal with Beautymist pantyhose that really raised eyebrows. What was a professional football player doing selling pantyhose? Making money. Plenty of it.

Joe was famous for a number of surgeries on his knees. A smart adman connected Joe's knees with the pantyhose. He figured it would draw tons of new female followers (to go along with the already large base of male fans).

In a Beautymist commercial filmed in 1974, the camera showed Joe in a reclining position looking straight at the camera, his elbow supporting his head. The camera pans straight up Namath's body until it reaches his face. Joe, obviously talking to women in the ad, tells them: "If the pantyhose makes my legs look good, how good do you think it will make your legs?" The ad was extremely controversial, especially for the time. The female audience sat up and took notice, and sales jumped. Beautymist

Matt Snell

The American Football League? Who?

An inferior league, not worth playing on the same field with the long-established National Football League.

Such was the thinking of many, including the NFL champion Baltimore Colts.

The New York Jets? A desperate team led by Joe Namath, their brash quarterback who had guaranteed victory in Super Bowl III.

Namath wasn't the only one on the Jets with a notion of pulling off a huge upset over the Colts. Matt Snell was about to make Namath's guarantee a fact.

Snell had an interesting distinction among the Jets. An Ohio State graduate, Snell was the first No. 1 draft choice the Jets (nee Titans) ever signed. He was the AFL's rookie of the year in 1964, led the team in rushing in five of his eight years with the Jets, and was an All-Pro. He teamed with Emerson Boozer to provide the Jets with one of the most devastating backfields in the pros. Once the game started, Snell and Boozer went about their business—the business of running the ball down Baltimore's throat.

The Jets had been warned to never run laterally against the Colts. They were too quick for them, it was believed. Namath paid no attention to that advice. At the line of scrimmage, Namath called a sweep.

"What I remember most was their bewilderment," Snell said of the Colts. "They couldn't believe we were doing it to them."

The Jets drove 80 yards to take a 7–0 lead on Snell's 4-yard run. They relied mostly on a play called "19 Straight."

"It was our bread and butter play with my lead block and Snell getting the ball," Boozer said." It worked all day long."

Snell pulled a muscle on the TD play. "I thought, 'How can I go the rest of the game?'" Snell said, "but it never got worse. And how was I to know it would be our only touchdown?"

Snell gained 121 yards on 30 carries. Namath completed 17 of 28 passes for 206 yards as the Jets won 16–7, humbling a Baltimore team that had lost only once the entire season.

sold a ton of pantyhose in one of the most successful product pitches in TV advertising history.

Namath, meanwhile, continued to live the high life with wine, women, and song. Once commenting on Namath's relationship with women, Dallas Cowboys quarterback Roger Staubach said: "I enjoy sex as much as Joe Namath. Only I do it with one girl."

Namath became a concern for the NFL when he invested in a nightclub, Bachelors III. Afraid the club might attract gamblers and other sordid types, the league forced Namath to sell his share.

Now, three days before Super Bowl III, Namath was at the Miami Touchdown Club to receive his award. In response to a heckler, Namath uttered those infamous words that became legendary: "The Jets will win on Sunday. I guarantee it."

His audience was stunned. His teammates were shocked. His coach was angry. "WHAT, ARE YOU CRAZY!" Jets coach Weeb Ewbank shouted. Namath said Jets tackle Dave Herman "wanted to choke me." Herman was going to face Bubba Smith, 6-foot-8 and 320 pounds of ferocity. "We don't need to excite him any more than he's going to be," said Herman.

Game time, and shockingly, the Jets took a halftime lead of 7–0 on a 4-yard TD run by Matt Snell and a great defense that intercepted Colts quarterback Earl Morrall three times deep in Jets territory. In the second half, Jim Turner kicked three field goals—32, 30, and 9 yards—for the Jets. It was all they needed to pull off perhaps the greatest of all football upsets, defeating the Colts 16–7.

Namath directed a steady offense that racked up 337 yards, including 121 yards rushing for fullback Snell. Namath was voted the game's MVP after completing 17 of 28 passes for 206 yards. Namath's teammates, who wanted to tear his head off after that shocking guarantee, now gave him the game ball. And Namath quickly handed it off to the NFL league office as a symbolic gesture. The AFL had finally come of age after a tumultuous struggle.

As for his guarantee, Namath said he was motivated by the outrageous odds against his team. "That's probably the reason I guaranteed we would win. Of course, it's one thing to say it and another thing to do it. We did it."

THE 1970S

Super Bowl IV

UNLIKE THE AFL'S SUPER BOWL QUARTERBACK OF THE PREVIOUS YEAR—
the guy with the long hair, longer fur coats, Broadway Joe nickname, and,
yes, big mouth—Len Dawson was eager to stay away from the spotlight.

As his Kansas City Chiefs prepared for the heavily favored NFL
champion Minnesota Vikings in the last Super Bowl before the full merger
of the leagues, Dawson had every reason to want to be anonymous.

Dubbed a journeyman after struggling with Pittsburgh and Cleveland in the established league—Dawson was a first-round draft pick by
the Steelers in 1957 out of pass-happy Purdue—he'd landed with the
AFL's Dallas Texans in 1962.

"And we won the championship," Dawson would quickly remind
everyone. "In double overtime in maybe the greatest championship game
ever."

But Dawson's work in that victory over the Houston Oilers was overshadowed by teammate Abner Haynes messing up the coin toss to begin
overtime. He was fine with that.

"I knew I was in the perfect place and I knew we could win more
championships," Dawson said. "With Hank [Stram] as our coach and
my familiarity with his offense and with Hank himself, I knew we would
succeed."

The Chiefs did, winning the 1966 league title, setting up a meeting with Vince Lombardi's Green Bay Packers in the first AFL-NFL
Championship; the game was not yet called the Super Bowl. With nearly
everyone projecting a Packers romp, Dawson was taken aback.

"We had so much talent that, yes, I was stunned at how people dis-
regarded us," he said.

But those people were correct. Dawson struggled against Ray Nitschke and company, throwing an interception, getting sacked six times, and falling 35–10.

Three seasons later, the Chiefs were back in the big game, and following the Jets' huge upset, at least they weren't treated like certain victims of the Vikings' Purple People Eaters.

But in the buildup to the game, Dawson was victimized by something more sinister: rumors he was involved with a gambling ring.

Several Chiefs games had been taken off the wagering boards during the 1968 and 1969 seasons for what authorities called "unusual betting patterns." Federal investigators alerted the NFL they had focused in on Dawson for his relationship with a gambler with the same last name: Donald "Dice" Dawson.

The league had launched its own investigation in '68 and Dawson "fully cooperated," according to NFL commissioner Pete Rozelle. But days before the kickoff against Minnesota, the NBC television network planned to air a report linking Dawson to a gambling ring.

"Hank called me aside to tell me about it, and I was stunned," Dawson said. "I knew [Dice Dawson], he'd called me during the season after my father had passed away. But there was nothing beyond that."

Rozelle and the league quickly found no basis to the NFL report—federal authorities hadn't even contacted the quarterback—and the Chiefs prepared a statement that Dawson read to the media in a late-night news conference. He explained his "casual" relationship with Dice Dawson, and that he'd never been "apprised of any reason why my name was brought up."

Not exactly the ideal way to prepare for any football game, let alone the Super Bowl. Dawson had been known for his unshakably calm demeanor on the field, but he'd been unnerved by the gambling reports and, on Super Bowl eve, he had a case of nausea. Ironically, those reports had caused some bettors to back the Vikings even more, and they entered the contest in New Orleans as 12½-point favorites.

Stram had put together a game plan featuring short passes, runs by tailback Mike Garrett, and several trick plays. The end-around would be a major weapon against the overly aggressive Vikings defense.

But he needed Dawson to be on his game.

"I can't say I was ever more focused or determined," Dawson said. "And I knew we were the better team."

The Chiefs were, from the outset. Masterfully, Dawson led them on drives to three Jan Stenerud field goals. Minnesota's intimidating defense that had yielded less than 10 points per game was, well, pedestrian against the Chiefs.

While Dawson worked over the Vikings, Stram marched along the sideline, rolled-up papers in his hand. Wearing a microphone for a subsequent NFL Films special, he was ecstatic with how his offense was toying with the Vikings, repeatedly mentioning: "65 toss power trap," a play the team hadn't even included in the game plan. Yet that became the Chiefs' signature running play on this day.

Still, it was the way Dawson responded to what could have been a chaotic lead-in to the game that had the most impact. The term "field general" often is used in reference to a quarterback's leadership. On this day, Dawson was the George S. Patton of the gridiron.

After Minnesota botched a kickoff return and Kansas City recovered, Dawson quickly moved his team toward the end zone. Garrett scored on a 5-yard run for a 16–0 halftime lead.

It wasn't really even that close.

Although the Vikings did get within nine points, Dawson and star receiver Otis Taylor hooked up against a blitz on a 46-yard catch and run down the right sideline for the final points of an emphatic 23–7 victory.

Years later, Dawson recalled that the overall significance of the win had escaped him moments after the final gun.

"The AFL had some outstanding teams and players, and when the merger came and we were going to begin playing [NFL teams] on a regular basis, we had won two Super Bowls, just like they had," he said. "But I really was thinking more about what we as a team had accomplished. We'd proven ourselves.

"There were no thoughts about vindication; nothing like that. My thoughts were simply that the Kansas City Chiefs were world champions."

Super Bowl V

"I'm a trivia answer," says former Dallas Cowboys linebacker Chuck Howley.

The question: Who is the only player to win the Super Bowl MVP award as a member of the losing team?

The answer: Chuck Howley.

Howley did it all for the Cowboys in Super Bowl V—everything but win the game. One of his two interceptions set up the first Cowboys field goal. The other in the end zone stopped a second-half Colts drive.

In another athletic play, Howley denied Baltimore's Tom Mitchell a touchdown pass on the final play of the first half. Then he combined with Lee Roy Jordan to force a fumble by Colts quarterback Johnny Unitas and set up the Cowboys' only touchdown of the day.

Oh, by the way, he also made three tackles.

Howley also keyed a defense that held the Colts to 69 yards rushing. To no avail. With five seconds left, Howley's Cowboys lost 16–13 on Jim O'Brien's 32-yard field goal.

Football wasn't the only sport that made Howley stand out. Howley was a man for all seasons at West Virginia, where he starred in five sports. He won varsity letters as a sprinter and weight man in track, a heavyweight in wrestling, a diver in swimming, and a trampolinist in gymnastics. Meanwhile, his college football teams compiled a 21-8-1 record during his three varsity seasons. He played offensive guard, linebacker, and center for the Mountaineers despite his smallish build at 6'2", 215 pounds. "I was a little guy," he acknowledged.

The Chicago Bears' No. 1 draft pick in 1957, his pro career appeared to be at an end when he suffered a serious knee injury in an exhibition

Jim O'Brien

In a mistake-filled game that would be dubbed the "Blunder Bowl," it was left to Jim O'Brien to get things right for the Baltimore Colts.

In the final seconds of Super Bowl V, the Colts and Dallas Cowboys were tied 13–13. On the Colts' sideline, rookie O'Brien was preparing for the kick that would decide a game in which the teams combined for 11 turnovers, and numerous fumbles and penalties. The Cowboys were penalized 10 times for 133 yards.

Earlier in the game, O'Brien had missed a PAT for the Colts, leaving them with a 6–6 tie.

"I was really nervous on that kick," O'Brien said. "It's like when you line up a three-foot putt. You're almost better if you have a 30-footer."

The Cowboys took a 13–6 lead into halftime. In the fourth quarter, the Colts answered with a TD. This time, O'Brien made the extra point.

With a minute to play, Colts linebacker Mike Curtis intercepted a pass by Craig Morton and brought the ball back to the Dallas 28. The Colts called a timeout with nine seconds remaining to set up O'Brien's kick.

The long-haired O'Brien stood by himself on the sideline, thinking, concentrating on the kick.

"Leave him alone," Jimmy Orr warned the other Colts. "Don't bug him."

Coach Don McCafferty had other ideas. He told quarterback Earl Morrall to talk to O'Brien. "Keep him calm," McCafferty said.

"Obie, we've got plenty of time," Morrall said.

"Is there a wind?" O'Brien asked.

"No wind. Just hit it for the middle."

Now was time for the 23-year-old O'Brien, who had been kicking game-winning field goals since he was eight years old, to trot onto the field.

game. "They kind of sent me home for a year," he said. Howley decided to retire from football and go into the service station business. "But then Dallas worked out a trade with the Bears and they asked me to play for the Cowboys," Howley said.

He was ready. On the way, Colts veteran Billy Ray Smith told O'Brien, "Kid, this kick is worth 300 grand to us ($7,500 a man). Don't mess up."

But O'Brien wasn't listening. He had dreamt all week that a field goal would win it. His mom, an astrologer, had called to say the stars were in the right order for the Colts to win.

He kept his mind a blank, learning from his previous extra point that was blocked, when O'Brien was thinking about things he shouldn't have been thinking about. "You should be on auto-pilot," said O'Brien.

The Cowboys were yelling for him to choke, to miss the kick. Concentrating, O'Brien tuned them out. "I remember concentrating very, very, very very hard, probably as hard as I've ever concentrated on a kick," said O'Brien.

Fans all over the country were waiting in suspense. O'Brien kicked high. The ball started right and then straightened out.

"I swear my heart had stopped beating," Morrall said. Colts linebacker Ted Hendricks, seated on the bench, turned away, afraid to watch.

O'Brien's 32-yard field goal sailed smoothly through the uprights, giving the Colts a 16–13 lead with five seconds left.

"It would have made it from 52, 53 yards out, if it would have had to," O'Brien said. "That one was one of the best I ever made."

The excited crowd of 72,204 at Miami's Orange Bowl erupted in cheers. O'Brien's ecstatic teammates rushed to congratulate him.

In a shocker, a player on the losing team, Chuck Howley, won the MVP award. The vote was already in before O'Brien made his winning kick. "The fact that Chuck Howley got it was appropriate considering it was a defensive battle and the guys were knocking each other around," O'Brien said.

O'Brien was the MVP hero as far as the Colts were concerned.

That he did. For 13 years, Howley was one of the top—and most feared—linebackers in the NFL.

"I wasn't afraid of too many people on game day," said safety Charlie Waters, who played with the Cowboys during the final four seasons of Howley's career. "But on game day I kept my distance from Chuck Howley."

The Cowboys led for most of Super Bowl V. They were ahead 13–6 entering the fourth quarter before giving up a touchdown. It stood at 13–13 until O'Brien came in to kick his 32-yard field goal as time expired.

Naturally, the loss was very hard to accept. It was even harder to accept what happened next. He had won the MVP award. All Howley could do was shrug his shoulders.

"It was hard to enjoy being MVP of that game," Howley said. "How do you celebrate that? I remember some of the other guys saying, 'Chuck, that's fantastic!' but it was very difficult to be enthusiastic." It meant a lot more to Howley a couple of weeks later when he was presented the award in New York.

Howley and his teammates didn't have to wait long to make up for their Super Bowl loss. The following year they won Super Bowl VI over Miami.

At 36, Howley was the oldest Cowboy playing that day in Super Bowl VI in New Orleans. Howley had one of his finest games. He recovered Larry Csonka's fumble—the first time the Miami fullback had turned over the ball that season—which led to a Dallas field goal and a 3–0 lead.

Once again, Howley was in the middle of the action with the Cowboys leading 17–3. He knocked down a Dolphins receiver and ended up on the ground himself. As Miami quarterback Bob Griese threw a pass, Howley jumped up and intercepted the ball, returning it to the Miami 9. Three plays later, the Cowboys scored to make it 24–3 and clinch the game.

The Cowboys didn't allow the Dolphins to score a touchdown. It was the only time in Super Bowl history that a team was held without a TD, and Howley certainly was a factor.

Super Bowl VI

HE WAS THE QUARTERBACK OF "AMERICA'S TEAM," "LIEUTENANT FAIR and Square," one of the most popular players in football history.

Roger Staubach took the long way around to become famous, serving as a naval officer in Vietnam for five years before making his mark in the NFL. At that point he was already 27 years old, at an age when many players had finished their careers in the league. (The average lifespan of a pro football player is less than five years.)

Playing for the Dallas Cowboys from 1969 to 1979, Staubach blossomed into an All-Pro quarterback with a knack for scrambling and delivering pinpoint passes.

One of his most famous was the "Hail Mary," a term that became popular when Staubach pulled out a game against the Minnesota Vikings in the 1975 playoffs. With a minute left, Staubach threw a 50-yard desperation pass to a well-covered Drew Pearson to give the Cowboys the victory.

Asked by a reporter what he was thinking when he threw the pass, Staubach replied, "I just closed my eyes and said a Hail Mary." Taking out a key chain, Staubach pointed to a tiny figure hanging from it.

"I've got the Blessed Virgin here," he said. "We're good buddies."

The Cowboys developed an ardent national following during Staubach's time in Dallas, even gaining the nickname "America's Team." Naturally it followed that Staubach would be known as "America's Quarterback"—and the target of mean-spirited opposing teams.

During one game, Staubach had the wind knocked out of him by a Philadelphia Eagles defender. While Staubach squirmed on the ground, the Eagles player said, "Take that, America's quarterback!" Instead, Staubach took the Cowboys to two championships.

For years, the Cowboys boasted the highest television ratings and sold more merchandise than any other team in the NFL. Meanwhile, Staubach was leading the Cowboys to five appearances in the Super Bowl, winning two. His performance in Super Bowl VI won him the MVP award.

Winning trophies was nothing new to Staubach, who had earned the Heisman Trophy at Navy.

Growing up in Cincinnati, Staubach started playing football in grade school. Not that his mother was very happy about it. She was anxious watching her son play. As Roger plunged into action, she would squeeze her rosary beads. She squeezed them so hard during the game that there were marks all over her hands.

Staubach started out as a running back and tight end, but his high school coach switched him to quarterback for his senior year. "They saw a vision that I didn't," Staubach told the *Cincinnati Enquirer*. That vision was filled with Staubach's scrambling ability. "If I hadn't been moved to quarterback," Staubach said, "my life would be different now."

As a high school senior, he was pursued by a handful of Big Ten schools. However, he chose the Naval Academy because it was "kind of romantic." In the 1960s, Staubach played on one of the last great Navy teams, leading the Middies as high as No. 2 in the rankings and just missing out on the national championship.

The Cowboys drafted Staubach in the 10th round in 1964, hoping he'd still have his skills when he became available.

Five years later, after his duty in Vietnam, Staubach began his pro career. He wasted little time in turning the Cowboys into one of the NFL's elite teams.

Along the way, he projected a clean-cut image. He refused to pose in an underwear advertisement he was offered. He turned down a cereal ad because the product had too much sugar. "God, family and country were always the priorities in Staubach's life," noted the *Boston Globe*.

After losing Super Bowl V, Staubach led the Cowboys to victory in Super Bowl VI over Miami in 1972. In that game, Staubach completed 12 of 19 passes for 119 yards and two touchdowns. The Cowboys held a 10–3 lead at the half before Staubach marched them 71 yards to set up a 3-yard TD run by Duane Thomas early in the third period. Chuck Howley's interception of a pass by Bob Griese set up another touchdown for the clincher.

Final score: Dallas 24, Miami 3.

"They looked like winners all the way on this cold afternoon (39 degrees) at Tulane Stadium before a crowd of 81,023," reported the *New York Times*.

The Cowboys' win capped a great second half of the season that featured 10 straight victories.

"We got in a groove where I do not think there was a team that ever played in the NFL that was better than we were from the middle of the season," Staubach told the *Palm Beach Post*. "We dominated most of those games."

DUANE THOMAS

Duane Thomas had everyone talking at Super Bowl VI. But he wasn't talking. The Dallas Cowboys' star running back was giving everyone the silent treatment.

He was at war with management over his contract. He went into his silent mode with anyone who crossed his path: the media, his teammates, and coaches.

On Super Bowl Monday, Thomas was surrounded by reporters waiting for an interview. When asked his first question, he answered, "I don't feel like being bothered now." After 15 minutes of absolute silence, Thomas asked what time it was. After 20 minutes, he left.

During meetings, he refused to answer to roll call. Awkward? Ya think?

"I was able to talk to him in the huddle," Cowboys quarterback Roger Staubach said. "He always practiced hard and he always played hard, so it wasn't a distraction." But he never spoke to Staubach off the field. "It was a little weird."

Steve Kiner, Thomas's onetime roommate, would tend to agree. "I roomed with him for a year and at the end I knew him as well as I know you," Kiner told a reporter for the *New York Times*.

Thomas, introverted and withdrawn, came from a broken home with a poverty-level upbringing. He was a high school standout in Dallas before starring at West Texas State and being selected by the Cowboys in the 1970 draft. He led the Cowboys in rushing with 803 yards, more than five yards a carry, despite not starting until the fifth game of the season. At the end of the season, he was voted Rookie of the Year in the National Football Conference.

He was being called the next Jim Brown, Cleveland's all-time great running back. With Thomas as one of the Cowboys' driving forces, they just missed winning Super Bowl V in 1971.

But the next year . . .

Even before the Cowboys showed up at Tulane Stadium, Thomas was already creating waves. He missed a team practice early in the week. Rumors were flying that Thomas didn't plan to play in the Super Bowl. It wasn't true—he showed up and paid his fine.

Missing practice was only part of his recalcitrant behavior. In warmup before games, Thomas would follow his own routine, apart from the rest of the players. Most of the players didn't mind, as long as he continued to perform brilliantly. "We didn't care what he did—but Tom did," said teammate Herb Adderley, a future Hall of Famer who was referencing Cowboys coach Tom Landry. Landry: "I tolerated him longer than most."

Thomas's brilliance seemed to overshadow his bad behavior.

In Super Bowl VI, the Cowboys dominated the Dolphins on the ground as they chalked up a Super Bowl–record at the time 252 yards rushing.

Leading 10–3 at the half, the Cowboys drove 71 yards to start the third quarter. Then Thomas scored on a 3-yard run, faking out two Dolphins, to make it 17–3. On the drive, Thomas rushed for 37 of his 95 yards.

The Dallas defense was just as good as its offense, holding the Dolphins without a touchdown, the first time that had happened in Super Bowl history.

Thomas's time had run out in Dallas after two short but brilliant seasons. Despite his great talent, the Cowboys traded Thomas to New England. His outrageous behavior soon left him without a job in football.

One of his stops, at least for a day or two, was San Diego. Thomas was fined and suspended for reporting late. He never got a chance to play for the Chargers.

"He wasn't warming up," coach Harland Svare told the *Times*. "He does things his own way. I made up my mind I didn't want that kind of a football team."

Yet coach Svare admitted that Thomas "had shown me even more talent than I expected he had."

At Super Bowl VI, Thomas was clearly the most valuable player with his slashing runs that left bodies all over the field. But the sports magazine that selected the MVP award winner decided to give it to quarterback Roger Staubach because of fears that Thomas would not make himself available for the media.

Thus Thomas, a rebel fighting management, had cost himself the award and the vehicle that went with it.

Super Bowl VII-VIII

Will the Miami Dolphins' record ever be broken?

Year after year, teams in the NFL strive for perfection—but so far no one has been able to match the Dolphins' perfect season of 1972.

That year, the Dolphins went 17-0 in winning Super Bowl VII, one of two straight championship seasons. Each year thereafter, Dolphins alumni from the '72 team have a celebration when the last undefeated team loses.

Through 2015, the string of breaking out the champagne remained intact for those Dolphins.

"We are the only team to ever go undefeated and we are—for some reason—not recognized for what we have done," said Garo Yepremian, the Dolphins' kicker from that game. "We weren't invited anywhere," Yepremian said.

The Dolphins never went to the White House. They didn't get a parade.

The Pittsburgh Steelers had "The Steel Curtain." The Los Angeles Rams had "The Fearsome Foursome." And the Minnesota Vikings had "The Purple People Eaters."

The Dolphins' defense was largely anonymous—so much so that Dallas Cowboys coach Tom Landry coined their nickname, "The No Name Defense."

How many of those aforementioned great teams went undefeated? Uh, none.

With a defense keyed by Jake Scott, a brilliant free safety and punt returner, the Dolphins beat the Washington Redskins 14–7 in Super Bowl VII. Scott won the MVP trophy.

Then, with fullback Larry Csonka winning the MVP award in the following Super Bowl, the Dolphins made it two straight with a 24–7 win over the Minnesota Vikings. It was, incidentally, an unprecedented at the time third straight appearance in the Super Bowl for an NFL team.

Coach Don Shula was understandably on edge as the team bus headed toward the LA Coliseum hours before Super Bowl VII. Perhaps he was thinking of his 0-2 Super Bowl record. He couldn't bear another loss.

According to The Associated Press, Scott was sitting a few rows back of Shula. "What are you worried about?" he needled the coach. "Are you worried that you're going to go down in the books as the losingest coach in Super Bowl history?"

"Shut up," Shula responded. "Get ready to play the game!"

Scott was ready, make no mistake. Playing despite an injury to his right shoulder and a bone chip in his wrist that needed surgery, Scott intercepted two passes, returning one 55 yards from the end zone.

"I was lucky on the first interception," Scott said. "I batted the ball in the air and caught it." On the second pass, Lloyd Mumphord and Scott were covering Charley Taylor. "[Washington quarterback Billy] Kilmer didn't see me coming across and the ball went right to me," Scott said. Meanwhile, he otherwise helped the "No Names" make a name for themselves, holding the Redskins without a point until the last two minutes of the game. It was only then that a botched play involving Yepremian (see sidebar) allowed the Redskins to get the game's final points.

Scott has been described as a free spirit who literally went his own way. As the Dolphins have celebrated their perfect season on a regular basis, Scott is the only player never to show up at reunions. He stayed out of the spotlight and rarely gave interviews. "He has just never been into self-promotion, and it has really hurt him in terms of recognition," former Dolphins teammate Jim Mandich once said. "This is a guy who for six or seven years played his position as well as it has ever been played."

Scott joined the Dolphins out of the University of Georgia in 1970 and played seven years with them before a trade to the Redskins. When he left the Dolphins, he was their all-time leader in interceptions (35) and punt return yardage (1,330 yards).

Teammates thought the world of him.

"If I had to be in a foxhole in a war and have somebody cover my backside, Jake would be my first choice," said safety Dick Anderson, who played alongside Scott in the backfield.

The foxhole analogy also might ring true of Csonka, the Dolphins' human battering ram at the fullback position. In Super Bowl VIII, Csonka was virtually the Dolphins' entire running attack with a Super Bowl–record 145 yards.

The NFL was built for parity, but apparently the Dolphins weren't aware of that as they made their third straight appearance in the big game, this time in Houston.

With Csonka at the heart of the Dolphins' ground attack, they put together a couple of long drives to take a 14–0 lead before the first quarter was over. The first drive was typical of the game plan.

"Csonka carried on five of the 10 plays for 36 of the 62 yards. He scored the touchdown from the 5 on a full-bore blast up the middle, Paul Krause and Jeff Siemon bouncing off him like handballs off the wall," reported the *New York Times*.

Csonka was one of Shula's favorite players, and no wonder. With Csonka blasting away at the line, the Dolphins forged one of the great power teams in NFL history. Csonka epitomized what the Dolphins of the 1970s were all about.

Because of his style, Csonka was constantly breaking his nose. After a while, he lost count. At one point, he had a special bar screwed onto his facemask to protect the nose. It didn't help much.

"In critical situations, you knew what Miami would do," said Merlin Olsen, the All-Pro defensive lineman for the Los Angeles Rams. "But even when you knew he was coming, he'd still get his yards. I don't remember any back in my 15 years in the league that was tougher to bring down."

Csonka developed his no-holds-barred style while playing at Syracuse University. Orange coach Ben Schwartzalder used him at linebacker as a sophomore.

"They thought I was too big to be a running back," Csonka said, "but then somebody got hurt and when I asked to be moved over to offense,

Garo Yepremian

The Miami Dolphins had just won Super Bowl VII. In the locker room, an unhappy Garo Yepremian, the Dolphins' placekicker, sat thinking about the game.

There were only two minutes left when Yepremian trotted onto the field to kick a 42-yard field goal. With the Dolphins leading the Washington Redskins 14–0, the game had long been decided. Yepremian, the tiny placekicker from Cyprus, was going to put the icing on the cake. The field goal would make it 17–0, completing a rare Super Bowl shutout.

Not so fast.

The kick was blocked and the ball bounced back toward Yepremian. He picked it up. Big mistake. The ball slipped out of his hands as he tried to pass. Another big mistake.

He batted it into the air where Washington's Mike Bass snatched it and ran almost untouched 49 yards for a touchdown.

Now it was 14–7 with still 2:07 left.

Deathly silence greeted Yepremian when he came back to the bench. Dolphins coach Don Shula snapped: "You should have fallen on the damn ball!"

Yepremian's teammate Bob Kuechenberg was angry.

"I mean, here we were out there, bleeding through every pore of our bodies and . . . I don't want to talk about it. I get too mad."

Other teammates felt the same.

The possibility for defeat after Yepremian's screw-up "made you sick even to think about it," said Jake Scott. The play followed Scott's second interception of a Billy Kilmer pass. Scott returned the ball from three yards deep in the end zone to Washington's 48. The Dolphins' drive stalled at the 34, leading to Yepremian's foul-up.

Despite Yepremian's misplay—and the angst it caused throughout South Florida—the Dolphins held on to win 14–7 behind their swarming defense.

It was little solace to Yepremian, whose bungled play has sometimes overshadowed his long career as a successful NFL kicker.

"There's not a day in my life that someone doesn't mention it," Yepremian said.

Ben agreed. Ben told me later that it would have been the worst mistake he ever made if he had kept me at linebacker. And once I got a chance to run, they never thought about moving me back to defense."

Before leaving Syracuse, Csonka had surpassed the rushing totals of some of the greatest running backs in college history, including Jim Brown, Jim Nance, and Floyd Little.

Drafted in 1968 by the Dolphins in the first round, Csonka took a few years to develop into a star. He gained more than 1,000 yards rushing in each of the Dolphins' three Super Bowl seasons, 1971–1973. He rushed for 112 yards in Super Bowl VII before breaking the Super Bowl record for yards with his 145 in Super Bowl VIII.

"He'd come off the field with his nose smashed, blood everywhere, in a terrible amount of pain, and you knew he'd be right back out there when we got the ball back," middle linebacker Nick Buoniconti said.

Csonka was on his way to the Hall of Fame.

Super Bowl IX-X

IT's EASY TO OVERLOOK LYNN SWANN'S PERFORMANCE IN SUPER BOWL IX. Terry Bradshaw did.

Swann, who would become a Hall of Fame receiver, didn't make a catch that day while the Pittsburgh Steelers were beating the Minnesota Vikings 16–6. As a matter of fact, Swann didn't remember the quarterback throwing anything his way at all. Bradshaw was too busy handing off to Franco Harris, who was the Super Bowl MVP that year, and passing to John Stallworth.

Bradshaw made up for his lack of attention to Swann the following year—big time. And the quarterback was happy that he did. All Swann did that day was make four catches and score a touchdown as the Steelers defeated the Cowboys 21–17 in Super Bowl X. Not just plain old, normal catches, but some of the most spectacular in Super Bowl history. Three of them were breathtaking. The first, according to Steelers public relations man Joe Gordon, "was one of the best I've ever seen." Swann caught the pass from Bradshaw two yards out of bounds, but somehow managed to bring the ball back just inside the sideline. The 32-yard play led to the Steelers' first TD.

Then came the second, a 53-yarder. Nicknamed "Nureyev" because of his ballet-like movements on the field, Swann used his supreme athleticism to leap over Dallas defensive back Mark Washington at the 49. He tipped the ball to himself at the 43, got up and was tackled at the 37. Although the incredible play didn't have an effect on the game, it has been considered one of the Super Bowl's greatest single plays.

The third headline-grabber was a long, arcing 64-yard touchdown pass to Swann in the fourth quarter that clinched the victory. Bradshaw was decked by Cowboys defensive lineman Larry Cole and didn't see Swann make his great catch.

Steelers cornerback Mel Blount did. "I was in disbelief," Blount said of Swann, who once studied ballet to help his footwork on the football field. "There was no way that physics would allow a guy to make some of those catches. All the plays he made, he was covered."

Remarkably, Swann made all those brilliant plays in the aftermath of a severe concussion he suffered in the AFC championship game. He was not even expected to play in the Super Bowl.

Swann, a No. 1 draft pick out of Southern Cal, joined the Steelers in 1974 just as they were perched to make a run as the most dominant team in football. In one six-year period, they won six division titles and four Super Bowl championships: IX, X, XIII, and XIV.

Bradshaw threw to Swann and Stallworth, as good as any one-two receiving pair in league history; Stallworth also made the Hall of Fame. Harris ran behind a strong offensive line featuring center Mike Webster. Both of them are in the Hall.

On defense, the "Steel Curtain" ruled with such players as "Mean" Joe Greene, Jack Lambert, and Jack Ham. Hall of Famers? You bet. Steel Curtain? You bet.

"I'd take our team and match them against anyone who ever played," Swann said.

Swann, in particular, had a habit of playing his best in the biggest games. He scored touchdowns in Super Bowl X, XIII, and XIV.

"For different reasons, every Super Bowl I played in was special to me," Swann told the *Austin American Statesman* in a 1999 interview. "For a lot of people in Pittsburgh, Super Bowl IX was the most important because it was our first, and it marked the beginning of the Steelers dynasty."

Swann made an impact in Pittsburgh almost from the moment he joined the team. He gave a hint of things to come when his touchdown catch in the AFC championship game against the Oakland Raiders was the deciding score.

On his way to the Canton shrine, Swann made 336 catches for 5,462 yards and 51 touchdowns in an era that did not emphasize the passing game. His outstanding performances in Super Bowl play were evident:

At the time of his retirement, Swann had compiled 363 receiving yards in four Super Bowls, ranking first in that category.

Harris won the Super Bowl IX MVP award by rushing for a record 158 yards on 34 carries. It's not what most Steelers fans remember first about his career, though.

No, Harris is forever tied to the "Immaculate Reception" in the 1972 AFC divisional playoff against the Oakland Raiders—generally regarded as the greatest play in NFL history.

The Steelers were trailing 7–6 with 22 seconds left, fourth-and-10 at their 40 yard line. One down left and 60 long yards to the Raiders' goal line.

Bradshaw had thrown three consecutive incomplete passes. Every one of the 50,000-odd fans in the stadium knew that another pass play was called for. But first Bradshaw had to escape the clutches of two bone-crushing linemen about to lower the boom on the Steelers QB. Flushed out of the pocket, Bradshaw looked downfield and spotted running back Frenchy Fuqua open for a split second. Bradshaw fired and fell.

And crossed his fingers.

The ball arrived in Fuqua's arms the same time that Jack Tatum clobbered him from behind. Tatum was nicknamed "The Assassin" for his ferocious hits that put many an NFL player out of commission.

"I could see Tatum," Fuqua said in an interview with The Associated Press many years later. "He had the reputation of a butcher and I could hear his footsteps and then I could hear him breathing, he was that close.

"Terry winged it, and I mean winged it." Among other qualities, Bradshaw was renowned for one of the strongest arms in the league.

Fuqua, trying to recover from Tatum's vicious hit, looked up to see Tatum smiling down at him. Suddenly Tatum's expression changed. Now he was wearing a frown.

"The ball had ricocheted 20 yards into the air, only to settle into Harris's hands at shoe-top height near the Raiders 42," the AP reported.

When he played at Penn State, Harris had been trained to "follow the ball . . . always go to the ball." Before he knew it, Harris had the ball come to him. Whether the play was legal is debated until this day; back then, two offensive players could not touch a pass consecutively. Then he turned toward the Raiders' goal line and blazed 40 yards for a touchdown.

The Steel Curtain

Minnesota's Purple People Eaters. Denver's Orange Crush. The New York Jets' Sack Exchange. All topped by Pittsburgh's Steel Curtain.

Pro football teams have had their share of colorful nicknames through the years, most of them on the defensive side. For sheer production, Pittsburgh's Steel Curtain outdoes them all with four Super Bowl championships.

In the 1970s, the Steelers ruled pro football with an awesome defense that started with a "mean" front four. That feared defensive line included Mean Joe Greene, L. C. Greenwood, Dwight White, and Ernie Holmes.

They became the Steelers' point of attack, the first dominant all-black starting four in NFL history. Featuring such colorful nicknames as Mean Joe, Hollywood Bags, Mad Dog, and Fats, the Steel Curtain hit as hard as anyone in the NFL.

They played with fiery intensity, screaming at opposing linemen. Once asked who hit harder on that line, Steelers running back Reggie Harrison said: "It all depends on what you prefer, Excedrin or Motrin. If you can find the rest of your body after they hit you, that's good."

There were other defensive stars on the team: Jack Lambert, Jack Ham, Mel Blount, and Andy Russell. The Steelers' offense wasn't too bad, either, featuring Franco Harris, Terry Bradshaw, John Stallworth, and Lynn Swann. The Steelers put it all together for wins in Super Bowls IX, X, XIII, and XIV.

A typical performance occurred in the 1975 playoffs when the Steelers beat Oakland for the AFC title, holding the Raiders to 29 yards rushing. The Minnesota Vikings didn't even reach that total in Super Bowl IX, when the Steel Curtain held them to 17 yards on 21 rushing plays, an average of 2.4 feet a carry.

Steel Curtain indeed.

"The only thing I could think of was, 'Get into the end zone. Don't even attempt a field goal, just get into the end zone.'"

He did, giving the Steelers a miracle of a 13–7 victory for their first postseason win. It was one of the most important triumphs in Steelers history. Next step: dynasty.

To say that it all started in Pittsburgh with Harris is not entirely true, but it is close enough.

"The first time I saw him run, he didn't look like a great runner," backfield mate Walter Abercombie told the *New York Times*. "Then I noticed how he glides by people, how he follows his blockers well, uses that little stutter step to get by one or two guys, and he turns a 2- or 3-yard gain into a 5- or 6-yard gain. The other thing I noticed is that he never takes a solid lick."

Harris's on-the-edge running style often took him out of bounds before a defender could lay a hand on him.

"I know he has been criticized over the years because he doesn't like to stick his head in there," Bradshaw said of the 6-foot-2, 225-pound running back, "but when he has to on a critical play—nobody sticks his head in there any farther."

Harris's running style perhaps explained the reason he lasted an amazing 13 seasons in the pros without serious injury. Running backs usually have a much shorter career than other players do in the NFL. As it was, Harris played in nine consecutive Pro Bowls from 1972 to 1980. When he retired, he had gained 12,120 yards and scored 100 touchdowns on his way to the Pro Football Hall of Fame.

At Penn State, Harris shared the backfield with Lydell Mitchell in perhaps the best pair of college running backs in the country. While Harris was piling up record rushing yardage, Mitchell had a solid, although less spectacular, pro career.

Harris, meanwhile, was quickly becoming one of the most popular players in Steelers history. His followers formed a "Franco's Italian Army" fan club. They came to games waving the Italian flag and wearing army helmets.

Bradshaw loved having him for a teammate. In a *New York Times* interview in 1983, when the two were in the same backfield for the last season, Bradshaw noted: "He's a Rolls-Royce, and since I haven't seen too many of them driving around the streets of Pittsburgh, it's nice to know there's one sitting right behind me on the field."

Super Bowl XI

THIS IS A TALE OF TWO FOOTBALL CITIES, AND ONE HARD-EDGED SPORTS genius. It's the story of Al Davis, a renegade (and visionary) football man who opened doors—and closed them just as quickly behind him.

"He was our first real success story," said George Ross, who was sports editor of the *Oakland Tribune* when Davis arrived in town to take over the Raiders in 1963.

Davis didn't take long to help the new team in town catch up with the San Francisco 49ers across the bay. He not only caught up with the 49ers, but surpassed them in many ways.

In a sense a super salesman, Davis got things done in a hurry. He sold the city of Oakland on a new stadium and sold the Raiders on themselves.

The year before Davis came to town, the Raiders were 1-13. In 1963, the Raiders improved to 10-4.

Wheeling and dealing at a ferocious pace, Davis collected 19 new players for the Oakland roster. In four years, Davis had the Raiders winning the American Football League championship. As onetime commissioner of the AFL, Davis was among the strongest voices to push through a merger with the NFL.

By the 1970s, the Raiders were among the winningest teams in all of football, one of the NFL's earliest dynasties after the merger.

With a sharp eye for talent, Davis brought in players, some of them castoffs, troublemakers, and misfits. He made them feel right at home in Oakland. And he made them champions.

He oversaw three Super Bowl victories (XI, XV, XVIII) and two losses (II, XVII) in fifteen years. Raiders players who wound up in the

Hall of Fame from those years included receiver Fred Biletnikoff, cornerback Willie Brown, tight end Dave Casper, offensive linemen Art Shell and Gene Upshaw, linebacker Ted Hendricks, running back Marcus Allen, and, of course, Al Davis himself.

When Davis came to town, the mood brightened considerably in Raiders camp. The Raiders had been mired in a culture of losing. "Davis came in and got it done," said Jim Otto, the longtime Raiders center and Hall of Famer.

Davis was born in Brockton, Massachusetts, the son of a garment manufacturer. He moved at an early age to Brooklyn, where he found an early sports hero in Jackie Robinson. When Robinson broke baseball's color line with the Dodgers, Davis was thrilled. He hoped that someday he could make such an impact himself.

But it was football, not baseball, where Davis would make his mark. Once asked when he knew he wanted to run a football team, he said, "When I was six."

Before long, he also knew that it was as a coach, not a player, that he would find his lifelong passion.

"I really wasn't much of an athlete," Davis once recalled. "I played a little football and baseball, but it would be inaccurate to say I starred or anything like that."

Later, that youthful desire would come to fruition when Davis as a coach helped Southern Cal win a national championship. He was also an assistant with the San Diego Chargers when offered the job of Raiders head coach.

Davis wanted complete control of the team, or as he had put it, "enough time and money to build the Raiders into a professional football team." That meant not only the coaching job but also the general manager role. In other words, no interference from the owners.

Ross sat in on a late-night session while Raiders owners Wayne Valley and Ed McGath were interviewing Davis. At that time, the Raiders were members of the AFL battling to survive against the NFL. Ross on Davis: "He was especially impressive discussing general manager functions and had at his fingertips a proposed budget for the 1963 season."

The next night, Ross had dinner with Davis. "He was especially interested in the support of the *Oakland Tribune*. I told him we were all going in the same direction." Ross added a footnote: "That didn't mean we wouldn't point out any flaws if there were any."

Davis said he had to be convinced, "as strongly as possible, that the club would remain in Oakland and would play in a new coliseum. Mr. McGath and Mr. Valley had a lot of stamina and convinced me we had a home in Oakland that was going to be permanent."

Ross: "Davis was the first to realize Oakland could have its own following. Others thought that the Raiders would just get the spillover from the 49ers. But Davis realized there were enough people in Oakland to develop a hardcore following." Put a good product on the field, and the fans will follow, Davis reasoned.

Now Davis was in a position to build a powerhouse. At the age of 33, he became the youngest coach and general manager in football history.

Davis wasn't kidding when he said he wanted complete control. That included the color of the Raiders' uniforms. He didn't particularly like the gold and black and wanted to make changes.

"I know he was enamored of Army's so-called 'Black Knights,'" Ross said. "Black and silver looked more ominous than the other uniforms they had." Black and silver it was, and that became an iconic color combination. It went perfectly with the pirates' double shield and eye patch.

As the wins came, so did the fans. The following deepened. All over town, Raiders bumper stickers sprouted. Enthusiasm even spread across the bay. Fans in San Francisco actually wanted to trade tickets with Oakland fans.

Suddenly, the Raiders were developing a personality of their own. And that personality was starting to overpower other AFL teams.

In the early years, Davis made sweeping changes, just about everyone from the front office to the water boy. And he made trades, lots of them. Among the first and most important was for quarterback Daryle Lamonica, whom Davis obtained from the Buffalo Bills.

"We were willing to wait a couple of years for Daryle," Davis said. "We knew it would take time to fit into our system. We knew we could play defense and we knew we could run the ball, but it was up to Daryle to get the passing game going."

Davis didn't have to wait long. In 1967, Lamonica's first year with the Raiders, he broke all team passing records. The Raiders went 13-1 before beating Houston in the AFL championship game and advancing to the Super Bowl. He was nicknamed "The Mad Bomber" for his long-range passing skills.

Lamonica was supported by a strong offensive line: guard Gene Upshaw, who had established himself as one of the AFL's best blockers, tackles Harry Schuh and Bob Svihus, center Jim Otto, guard Wayne Hawkins, and tight end Billy Cannon.

Working with Lamonica in the Oakland backfield were running back Clem Daniels and fullback Hewritt Dixon.

Before 1967, the Raiders' main deficiency on offense was at wide receiver. This Davis took care of with the acquisition of Bill Miller and Warren Wells and the continued maturation of Biletnikoff, destined to become the MVP of Super Bowl XI.

Defensively, the Raiders were as deep as any team in the league. Dave Grayson, an all-AFL performer, and Kent McCloughan, two tough and fast players, were among the cornerbacks. The Oakland safeties included Howie Williams and Roger Bird, who doubled as the punt return specialist.

On the defensive line were two giants for their time at each end, 6'7", 265-pound Ben Davidson, and 6'5", 270-pound Ike Lassiter. Dan Birdwell and Tom Keating were small but quick tackles and the line worked beautifully together.

"They had an all-out offense, bombs to Wells, Biletnikoff and Cannon. And they had an aggressive defense, set a record for most sacks in a season," said Glenn Dickey, who covered the Raiders for the *San Francisco Chronicle*.

"Just win, baby," became one of Davis's most popular expressions.

The Raiders did. But they also developed a dark image for themselves—and their fans, who turned the Oakland Coliseum into the self-proclaimed black hole. Not that Davis cared. The Raiders were among the roughest teams in the league, some said the dirtiest. One of

Fred Biletnikoff

"I was no gazelle!"

—Fred Biletnikoff

When you make a great catch in a Super Bowl game, your teammates usually cheer and give you a high-five.

Fred Biletnikoff returned to startling silence after he made a key 48-yard catch in Super Bowl XI. No cheers. No high-fives.

"They didn't have to say anything," Biletnikoff said. "I knew what they were thinking. I told coach I ran as fast as I could."

But it wasn't fast enough, and Biletnikoff was caught from behind—a common problem for the slow-footed receiver. His teammates knew it only too well.

"They just ran me down," Biletnikoff said after the big play brought the Raiders to Minnesota's 2 yard line. "But I was just happy to hang on to the ball. I knew once we got that close, we'd be able to score."

Perhaps fittingly, Biletnikoff's pro football career got off to a slow start. As a rookie in 1965, he only caught 24 passes for 331 yards and no TDs.

Though not exceptionally fast, Biletnikoff had made an impact on the Florida State football program with his sure-handed pass-catching ability. In the 1965 Gator Bowl, Biletnikoff caught four touchdown passes to lead Florida State to victory over Oklahoma. Davis signed Biletnikoff to a pro contract under the goalposts before a national TV audience.

"Fred had such great hands, and although he wasn't a sprinter, he had quick moves in the final stages of receiving," Florida State coach Bill Peterson said.

Knowing he lacked speed, Biletnikoff went to extremes in his work ethic. He was first in the Raiders' locker room and undaunting in his practice schedule. He never gave up, never satisfied until he felt he had perfect catches.

Things got better when quarterback Daryle Lamonica joined the Raiders and made Biletnikoff one of his favorite targets. Then Lamonica was replaced by Kenny Stabler and the passes kept floating Biletnikoff's way.

And by 1977, the Raiders had advanced to Super Bowl XI to face the Minnesota Vikings.

"We knew we could move the ball on the Vikings, so we only threw it as much as we had to," Biletnikoff said. "It was just a matter of Stabler getting back there and reading the defense. Whoever was getting open, that's who was getting the ball."

Biletnikoff figured he could handle Minnesota cornerback Nate Wright in single coverage. When the Vikings expected a running play, Biletnikoff ran a post pattern and made a sliding catch at the 1. "I had to come out of the end zone, because Stabler led me away from the coverage," Biletnikoff said.

Dave Casper scored on a pass from Stabler to give the Raiders a 10-0 lead. Next, Biletnikoff made a 17-yard reception with a sliding catch at the goal line. Pete Banaszak took it across. Halftime score: Oakland 16, Minnesota 0.

Biletnikoff finished his day's work by hooking up with Stabler on that 48-yard catch in the middle of the field. Biletnikoff lugged the ball to the 2, setting the stage for Banaszak's second TD of the day.

"We knew the safety, Paul Krause, was going to be around there someplace," Biletnikoff said. "Kenny threw the ball low, so it wouldn't get picked off. I was just hoping to be there when the ball got there."

It was one of four catches for Biletnikoff totaling 79 yards, as the Raiders defeated the Vikings 32–14. Although Biletnikoff didn't score any touchdowns, three of his catches moved the ball to the shadow of the goal line and were converted into TDs.

Biletnikoff did just about everything for the Raiders but get into the end zone. As it was, he came very close, totaling four yards short of three scores. "I got my fingers as close to the goal line as I could," Biletnikoff said.

Biletnikoff won the Super Bowl MVP trophy. He didn't think it was right.

"A stick of gum would have been enough," Biletnikoff said of the MVP trophy. "I was surprised to hear that I had won it. It's like all the rest of the guys got cheated. That makes me feel bad. The feeling that makes me happy is that we won."

The "slow" receiver became known as one of the top pass catchers in pro football history. He was inducted into the Hall of Fame in 1988.

the most talked about was Davidson, whose nasty reputation put him at the top of the Raiders' opponents' hit list. "He even got [blamed] for things he didn't do," Dickey said. "It was all part of his 'dirty' image."

The Raiders enjoyed playing the role of villain, reflecting their owner's bad-boy image. They developed a rough-and-ready style known for their over-the-line, edgy play.

With his win-at-all-costs philosophy, Davis didn't care how many crimes his players committed on the field as long as the team played well. And just won, baby!

Meanwhile, Davis became famous for his ability to resurrect the careers of players, most notably George Blanda, who signed with the Raiders in his 40s after a long and notable career in the AFL. Davis also found other players who had either gone bad or lost favor with their teams, but in Oakland found a home.

Davis would be the Raiders' face of the franchise for decades. He was the team's principal owner and general manager from 1972 to 2011, including a 12-year stint in Los Angeles. Davis gave the NFL no little aggravation in winning a court battle that allowed him to move the team to Los Angeles in 1982. Then he returned to Oakland in 1994, causing even more distress for the NFL. His legal battles with the league became legendary.

In trying to move the Raiders to Los Angeles, he was first blocked by a court injunction in 1980. Two years later, he filed an antitrust suit against the NFL and was successful when a district court gave the move a green light. In 1995, unable to get a state-of-the-art stadium built, Davis decided he had enough of L.A. and returned to Oakland.

Off the field, the iconoclastic Davis was active in civil rights. He refused to allow the Raiders to play in any city where blacks and whites had to stay in separate hotels.

There was hardly a season gone by that Davis didn't do something to shake things up in the NFL. He was the first NFL owner to hire an African-American coach (Art Shell) and the second to hire a Latino (Tom Flores). He was also the first to make a woman the chief executive on his team (Amy Trask).

Davis had a unique perspective on football from just about any view: assistant coach, head coach, GM, and owner. He was even a commissioner for a while when he took charge of the American Football League for a year in 1966.

Mike Berger, onetime editor of the *San Francisco Chronicle*, remembers he was a young reporter when he first ran into Davis.

"You could be charmed by him, or put off," Berger recalled. "It all depended on how he sized you up. If you asked him tough questions, he might bark, but he would respect you.

"[The Raiders] were very sensitive about comparisons with the NFL at that time. I had several run-ins with him over it, but I felt there was mutual respect there. He was exceptionally bright. He loved to probe and test people, an altogether interesting man."

Super Bowl XII

ORANGE CRUSH VS. DOOMSDAY DEFENSE.

No contest.

Before the Denver Broncos started winning Super Bowls in the 1990s, there were the Dallas Cowboys showing how to do it in the 1970s and 1980s. The Cowboys were led by their famous Doomsday Defense featuring a front four of Randy White, Harvey Martin, Ed "Too Tall" Jones, and Jethro Pugh.

In an unprecedented selection by sportswriters, White and Martin shared the MVP award in Super Bowl XII. The duo made a painfully effective impact as the Cowboys defeated the Broncos 27–10. The Broncos, known as the Orange Crush after the popular soft drink of the day and the color of their uniforms, ran into a powerful attack from the Cowboys.

"Orange Crush is soda water," Martin said after the game. "You drink it. It didn't win football games."

White and Martin, in particular, caused all kinds of problems for Denver quarterback Craig Morton, a former Cowboy. "All I remember about the game is that Harvey and Too Tall and Randy White were in our backfield more than I was," Morton said.

"Denver was looking for the blitz," Martin said. "We showed it to them, but we used just good defensive football. We wanted to give Morton something to think about, but it was just four guys rushing the passer."

A Texas native, Martin played his college ball at East Texas State (now Texas A&M Commerce). He led Commerce to the NAIA national championship in 1972 and wound up a third-round draft choice of the Cowboys in 1973.

Before joining the Cowboys, Martin got some tips from a former college teammate, Dwight White. White and Joe Greene, members of the Pittsburgh Steelers' famous Steel Curtain defensive line, took rookie Martin to a park in Grand Prairie, Texas, and taught him a few tricks. "Tricks like how to make the move inside after faking to the outside, how to turn the offensive lineman so his own momentum carries him past you," Martin said. After two months, he went to camp with an edge over the other rookies.

Even so, as a rookie, Martin was in danger of being cut. He was told he was "too nice." Drew Pearson, the Cowboys' outstanding wide receiver, remembered, "Harvey changed overnight. All of a sudden, Too Nice became Too Mean." He became Dallas's sacks leader.

In the 1977 Cowboys' media guide, Martin described his pass-rush technique: "Combine speed with 250 pounds and squeeze."

Commerce teammate Sam Sterling thought Martin really developed into a star in college. "More than anything, it was a place for him to grow up and learn how to play football," Sterling said. "When he got to [East Texas State], he really more or less grew up with the team."

Martin's teammate, Hall of Famer Randy White, will be remembered as one of the greatest linemen in Cowboys history—held in the same respect as Bob Lilly, Lee Roy Jordan, and Jethro Pugh.

When White held out for a new contract in 1984, his teammates were unhappy with management. To show their displeasure, they cut off the colored tops of their sweat socks and wrote White's number 54 on them. They wore them as armbands of mourning. To further emphasize their message, taped across the back of their helmets was the note, WHERE'S RANDY? The correct answer, of course: fishing. White was known as an avid fisherman.

White missed all of training camp but didn't miss a beat in the season's opener. The Los Angeles Rams were driving for a touchdown in the last three minutes. With the ball on the Dallas 29, White broke through a double-team on a fourth-and-1 and stopped the play cold.

"The Manster is back," said John Dutton, the Cowboys' other defensive tackle. Manster? As in half man, half monster, a nickname teammates had given him.

"When I came to the Cowboys, I had heard all the hype about Randy," Jim Jeffcoat said. "But it wasn't hype. It was all true. When he was in, you never had to worry about him taking off a play. There was no one in the league like him."

Before winning Super Bowls, White was winning individual trophies in college at Maryland. In 1974, he won the Outland Trophy as the best college lineman in the country.

White has always loved the competitive nature of sports, and it's obviously a family trait—starting with his mother. Once, while White was playing a high school football game in Wilmington, Delaware, a fight broke out in the stands. He quickly recognized one of the figures in the fight: Mom! "She was using her umbrella on a guy," White remembered.

Morton must have felt just as victimized as he was being battered by the Cowboys' front four in Super Bowl XII. "We knew we had to pressure Morton," White said. "It was part of our game plan. I figured that if we didn't give them turnovers and [good] field position we would win." That's just what happened. The Cowboys gave the Broncos good field position only three times, and stopped them on two of those occasions.

"It seemed as though Morton was looking at me every time he came to the line," Martin said. "I think he was more concerned because he thought all of us would be coming at him."

Going into Super Bowl XII, the Cowboys had the No. 1 defense in the NFL. They showed why in the lopsided contest in New Orleans.

Led by White and Martin, Dallas hammered Morton into submission. Morton was forced to spend the fourth quarter on the bench. Martin had one of his biggest days with two sacks and a pass deflection. White added enormous pressure on Morton, forcing him to throw four interceptions. The Broncos had four other turnovers. The Cowboys held the Broncos to 156 total yards, including just 35 passing yards.

Cowboys quarterback Roger Staubach, meanwhile, took care of the other side of the ball. His key play: a 45-yard touchdown pass to a diving Butch Johnson.

The game featured a slew of Super Bowl firsts: the first Super Bowl indoors; the first played in prime time; and the first time two players shared the Super Bowl MVP award: White and Martin.

Super Bowl XIII-XIV

QUARTERBACKS HAVE A TOUGH JOB.

Because they handle the ball more than anyone, they usually are the first to be praised or blamed by critics.

After a terrible rookie year with the Pittsburgh Steelers in 1970, Terry Bradshaw was ready to take all of the blame for that season. And his teammates would agree with him.

"My rookie year was a disaster," said Bradshaw. "I had never studied the game, never looked at films the way a quarterback should. I had never been benched before. I'd never even played on a team that had another quarterback besides me. I had no idea how important I was to the team."

Believe it or not, Bradshaw had never seen the Steelers play on television. After his rookie season, he was discouraged, but not defeated. In the offseason, he started to prepare himself.

The Steelers would soon be winning Super Bowls—four, in fact. And Bradshaw, who felt brutally inept as a rookie, was soon winning MVPs in the Super Bowl—two, in fact.

When Bradshaw joined the Steelers in 1970, a lot was expected of him. After all, he was the No. 1 pick in the NFL draft after completing a marvelous college career at Louisiana Tech.

The Steelers needed a quarterback who could shred defenses with his powerful arm, as Bradshaw had done in small-college football with more than 7,000 yards. Stories persisted about this rocket-armed quarterback who could throw the pigskin practically the length of the field.

Bradshaw developed that arm in part as a javelin thrower in high school in Shreveport, Louisiana, where he set a number of track-and-field records. In college, he caught the eye of pro scouts with his record-setting ways.

The Steelers were desperate: In 35 years, they had never won a championship of any kind. The season before, they managed only one victory in 14 games. The Steelers first started to turn the corner with the hiring of coach Chuck Noll in 1969, although the 1-13 record was the same as the previous year.

With a number of high picks available because of the Steelers' poor history, Noll picked some prizes out of the next few drafts—many of them, it turned out, future Hall of Famers. Bradshaw was among them.

The draft picks read like a Who's Who in college football history. Try these: "Mean" Joe Greene, Bradshaw, Mel Blount, Jack Ham, Franco Harris, Mike Webster, Lynn Swann, John Stallworth, and Jack Lambert. This group comprised one of the greatest dynasties in pro football history.

Bradshaw had the talent to be the Steelers' savior at quarterback. But first he had to overcome one of the worst chapters in Steelers history.

Bradshaw had to first prove himself to a bunch of hardened veterans. He had difficulty relating to his teammates with his country ways and Bible Belt philosophy. "I was an outsider who didn't mingle well," said Bradshaw. "There were no cowboys on the team, no one who liked to fish or do the things I liked to do. The other players looked upon me as a Bible-toting Li'l Abner."

Embarrassing—that would be a good way to describe Bradshaw's rookie season. He completed only 38 percent of his passes. He threw a grand total of six touchdown passes and was intercepted 24 times. What a stinker! Only one positive note: the Steelers went from a 1-13 record to 5-9, their best record since 1966.

If Bradshaw was disappointed with his first pro season, the same couldn't be said of Noll and the rest of the Steelers coaching staff. After all, they had improved their record dramatically and had great belief in Bradshaw's talents.

In the offseason, Bradshaw went home and started working ferociously on his game. He had lost his confidence, but soon started to get it back. "All I could think about was, 'I'll show 'em.' In that offseason, I worked and worked."

John Stallworth

It was 1982, and another classic matchup between the Pittsburgh Steelers and Dallas Cowboys.

Early in the game, Steelers receiver John Stallworth went downfield on a passing route. Cowboys cornerback Dennis Thurman gave Stallworth a vicious forearm to his head when the ball was away from them.

Stallworth sank to his knees. He pointed at Thurman. "You can't cover me," Stallworth said. Stallworth caught two more passes.

Thomas whacked Stallworth again on a pass into the end zone. Stallworth was forced to leave the game.

When he came back for the next series, Stallworth caught a 25-yard pass from Terry Bradshaw,.

Stallworth pointed at Thurman again. "You still can't cover me." The Steelers defeated the Cowboys 36–28.

That display was typical of Stallworth, the other half of the Steelers' incomparable pass-catching duo along with Lynn Swann. They helped to win four Super Bowls for the Steelers—Super Bowls IX, X, XIII, and XIV.

Growing up in the shadow of the University of Alabama, Stallworth was ignored by Crimson Tide coach Bear Bryant, who had integrated the team the year before. "They were taking only the elite of the elite," Stallworth said.

Stallworth ended up at Alabama A&M under coach Louis Crews, who took one look at his 6-foot-2, 167-pound frame and dubbed him "Spaghetti."

Stallworth loved it there and got lots of playing time, but little publicity. "Hindsight is always 20-20, but I could have been lost in the shuffle at Alabama," Stallworth said. "They weren't throwing the ball a lot in those days."

It paid off. Bradshaw had a strong second season, and except for a few missteps, the Steelers continued to improve throughout the 1970s. Growing along with Bradshaw were such top offensive players as Stallworth, Swann, Harris, Rocky Bleier, and the legendary Steel Curtain defense.

He was drafted by the Steelers in the fourth round of the 1974 NFL draft. Hampered by injuries, he had a slow start. But in his second year, he stepped into the lineup and so dominated the Steelers' passing offense that he was still there 13 years later.

Many of his phenomenal catches were worthy of highlight reels. Among his 537 receptions and 63 touchdown catches were several brilliant plays he made in Super Bowl competition.

In Super Bowl XIII versus Dallas, he made scoring catches of 75 and 28 yards in the first half, then collapsed in the locker room with leg cramps. The Steelers went on to win, 35–31.

"The bigger the game, the better the catch," said Texas Southern University coach Lionel Taylor, a Hall of Fame receiver himself. "That's what separates him."

In Super Bowl XIV, the Steelers were trailing the Los Angeles Rams 19–17 when Steelers coach Chuck Noll called quarterback Terry Bradshaw over for a meeting.

"You're not going to pick your way against the Rams," Noll said. "Go for the big play."

That meant Stallworth. The lead had changed five times. Then came the decisive call. The Steelers' play was known as "60 prevent, slot, hook and go." On third-and-8 at the Steelers 27 yard line, Stallworth took two defenders 15 yards downfield, hooked, and then went deep, catching a Bradshaw pass 39 yards from the line of scrimmage. Stallworth raced the remaining 34 yards for a touchdown that gave the Steelers the lead for good. Stallworth made three key receptions for 121 yards, including the 73-yard touchdown pass.

Along with winning four Super Bowls, Stallworth was voted All-Pro. But he was really excited when his Steelers teammates voted him MVP in 1979.

"There are so many super players on this team," Stallworth said. "And if they think you're the MVP, it really matters. Then you've really made it."

The Steelers finally reached the top of the football world for the first time with a 16–6 victory over Minnesota in Super Bowl IX. Then the Steelers made it two in a row with a 21–17 triumph over Dallas in Super Bowl X.

After an absence of two years, the Steelers returned to the Big Game. Bradshaw was at his best as the Steelers defeated the Cowboys 35–31 and the Los Angeles Rams 31–19 for their fourth Super Bowl victory in six years—still unprecedented. Bradshaw won the MVP award in each of the last two Super Bowls.

Did someone say dynasty? That's what everyone was saying about this Steelers team.

In the second victory over the Cowboys, Bradshaw threw four touchdown passes. He connected twice to Stallworth and once to Bleier to help the Steelers take a 21–14 lead at intermission. After the Cowboys kicked a field goal to cut Pittsburgh's lead to 21–17 in the second half, Harris scored on a 22-yard gallop and Bradshaw connected with Swann on an 18-yarder to make it 35–17.

The game seemed to be just about over at that point. At least before Roger Staubach went to work. With less than three minutes to go, the Cowboys quarterback threw two TD passes to cut Pittsburgh's lead to four points. The Cowboys tried an onside kick. It failed, and the Steelers hung on to win their third Super Bowl. Bradshaw finished with 17 completions in 30 passes for 318 yards in one of the most exciting Super Bowl games ever.

"The thing I didn't want to do was change what got me here," Bradshaw told the *Palm Beach Post*. "I wanted to stick to the play-action passes—Franco [Harris] running the ball—the things we had success with all season. I wasn't going to come in here and let the hoopla of the Super Bowl dictate to me the kind of game we played."

Same might be said of Super Bowl XIV against the Los Angeles Rams.

It was a record-breaking performance by Bradshaw, who was 14 of 21 for 309 yards. Bradshaw passed for two TDs, giving him a record at the time of nine in Super Bowls. He also increased his record total yards in Super Bowl competition to 932. Meanwhile, the Steelers as a team won that fourth Super Bowl—another record at the time.

They put themselves into a position to win when Bradshaw lofted a 73-yard scoring pass to Stallworth in the fourth quarter. That put the Steelers in front to stay, 24–19.

"That was against the prevent defense on third down," Bradshaw said proudly.

He said the victory was his most satisfying Super Bowl. "We had a chance to set some history, and we did it."

Bradshaw had taken the Steelers from doormat to dynasty.

THE 1980s

Super Bowl XV

How do you resurrect a dead football career? Win a Super Bowl.

The future had looked grim for Jim Plunkett. Cut by the San Francisco 49ers in 1976, he was on the verge of forced retirement. "They said Jim didn't have it anymore," said Oakland Raiders receiver Cliff Branch.

The Raiders thought differently. Raiders owner Al Davis was a maverick who liked to take chances, having resurrected many football careers in Oakland. He took a chance on Plunkett. That didn't mean Plunkett was going to play. Plunkett didn't play a single down for the Raiders in 1978. In 1979, he threw just 15 passes. Was it time to retire? Somehow he hung on.

"When this year started, I was disappointed and upset," Plunkett said in 1979. "Prior to the season, I thought about hanging it up."

A few of his friends convinced him things would work out. He wasn't so sure.

"I had been on top for so long," Plunkett said. "I don't know how I got through all the low spots that followed in the pros. I would get defensive and depressed and down on myself."

In Oakland, Plunkett sat behind Dan Pastorini, an old rival. They both were star quarterbacks in California high schools, coming out the same year. Plunkett was recruited by Stanford, Pastorini by Santa Clara. Plunkett earned All-America honors while Pastorini made the Little All-America team.

Plunkett was the top draft choice in 1971 by the New England Patriots after winning the Heisman Trophy, Pastorini the third overall by Houston. Now Pastorini was the Raiders' No. 1 quarterback, and Plunkett was the backup. Plunkett was not happy with that arrangement—particularly since he had outplayed Pastorini during the exhibition season. So one day in training camp, he approached coach Tom Flores and asked to be traded or released. He wanted a chance to play elsewhere.

Though he started the 1980 season on the bench again, everything was about to change. Fate was on Plunkett's side: In the fifth game of the season, Pastorini broke his leg. Immediately Plunkett became the leader. "Jim just came into our huddle and ran the show," Branch said.

He ran it so well that the Raiders made it to Super Bowl XV and a date with the Philadelphia Eagles. It wasn't an easy route the Raiders took to get to the NFL's big game. As a wild-card team, they had to win three games on the road before the Super Bowl. In the AFC championship game against San Diego, the Raiders had clinched it by holding on to the ball for almost seven minutes at the end.

The Raiders and Eagles had tangled twice earlier in the season, Oakland winning an exhibition game at home while the Eagles won a regular-season game in Philadelphia. The Eagles were three-point favorites in the Super Bowl, which was billed as a morality play, "good vs. evil," in some eyes. The Eagles represented conservative America, the Raiders, the league's "bad boys," reflecting the attitude of their owner.

"We're not a bunch of choir boys and boy scouts," said Raiders left guard Gene Upshaw. "They say we're the halfway house of the NFL. Well, we live up to that image."

As the Raiders stepped off the plane upon their arrival in New Orleans for the Super Bowl, they were full of confidence. "Watch this game carefully," offensive tackle Henry Lawrence told reporters. "Last time they did things to us that they won't do this time. They stopped our running, but they won't do it Sunday. They won't get to Plunkett."

The last time they played, the Raiders' offensive line gave up eight sacks to the Eagles. This game, they gave Plunkett much more time to work his magic.

The highlight of the game for the Raiders came in the first quarter, from their 20 yard line, third-and-4. Plunkett dropped back and looked for receiver Bobby Chandler cutting across the middle. Chandler was covered, so Plunkett ran to his left. He spotted halfback Kenny King

Rod Martin

Rod Martin had super bad timing.

In Super Bowl XV, he had an historic game. Martin intercepted a Super Bowl record three passes as the Oakland Raiders beat the Philadelphia Eagles 27–10.

He did not receive the MVP trophy for his extraordinary achievement. That award went to quarterback Jim Plunkett, making a dramatic comeback when his career seemed all but finished.

Later on, in Super Bowl XVIII, Martin keyed a strong defense to help the Raiders whip the defending world champion Washington Redskins 38–9. Martin's contribution that day included a sack, a fumble recovery, and a key pass breakup in the second quarter. He also made a key stop of the Redskins' star fullback John Riggins, the previous year's Super Bowl MVP, on a big fourth-and-1.

No one seemed to notice: Marcus Allen had a Super Bowl–record 191 yards rushing and two touchdowns. Once again, no MVP for Martin, which he found unbelievable.

"How can the person who intercepted those passes not be named the MVP?" Martin said. "I still can't understand it."

Martin felt he and Plunkett could have shared the award. "I think Jim even feels the same way," Martin said.

The snub may have made Martin a better player. "It made me, a little 12th-round draft choice, want to play harder and prove everybody wrong."

He was voted AFC Defensive Player of the Year in 1983 and made the Pro Bowl in 1983 and 1984. He became one of the best linebackers in Raiders history.

"I think I did prove to everybody that what I did in that Super Bowl was no fluke," Martin said.

Does Martin ever think his record three interceptions in Super Bowl XV will be broken?

"I don't know if the record will ever be broken, but I know it will not be broken by a linebacker," Martin said. "And for a defensive back to break it, they would have to keep throwing in his direction, which they wouldn't do if he was picking off all of their passes."

racing down the left sideline past defensive back Herman Edwards. Plunkett completed a pass to King and the running back was off on an 80-yard scoring play that at the time was the longest in Super Bowl history. The Raiders got the benefit of a no-call on a holding infraction, and the play stood for a 14–0 lead in the first quarter. It didn't matter either way as the Raiders scored 13 more points and defeated the Eagles 27–10. Plunkett was 13 of 21 for 261 yards and three touchdowns, and was voted the game's MVP. "If they didn't name him the Most Valuable Player, it would have been robbery," said Eagles defensive end Claude Humphrey. "There was no other MVP on the field today. It was him."

Plunkett was unimpressed. "I'm not playing any better now than I ever was," Plunkett said. "I'm playing with better people."

The game turned around Plunkett's career. He was not only recognized as the Comeback Player of the Year in 1980, but also added another championship to his resume in Super Bowl XVIII.

"I know how everybody trashed Jim Plunkett," Davis said. "They trashed him so hard they nearly broke him. But to me, Jim is like Rocky Marciano. He's going to swing, he's going to swing some more, and he's going to take some punches. But in the end, he's going to knock you out."

Super Bowl XVI

QUARTERBACK OF THE FUTURE OR JUST ANOTHER JOE? HE HAD AN inaccurate and inconsistent arm, according to NFL scouting reports on Joe Montana. During a portion of his career at Notre Dame, he was a seventh-string quarterback—barely. His skinny 6-foot-2, 196-pound frame wasn't impressive. So was this an NFL star in the making? Might be. Maybe even something more.

He certainly impressed Bill Walsh, general manager and coach of the San Francisco 49ers. Walsh became aware of Montana when he read about his exploits under impossible conditions in the deep-freeze Cotton Bowl game in 1979. The game was played under wintry conditions—an ice storm had blanketed the area the day before.

With Notre Dame trailing 34–12 in the final quarter, Montana—sick with fever—led a rally in freezing rain. With the nerveless quarterback showing the way, the Irish scored 23 points in seven minutes to win 35–34.

Montana capped the rally with a touchdown pass to split end Kris Haines with only two seconds on the clock, setting the stage for the winning extra point.

Walsh wasted no time in further scouting Montana. He checked out this cool, confident quarterback and liked what he saw. "The minute I saw Joe move, there was no question in my mind that he was the best I'd seen," Walsh said. "I know the offense I planned to run, Joe would be great."

Following his basic football instincts, Walsh drafted Montana in the third round in 1979. That meant 81 prospects were selected before Walsh made his move. "Joe's not an intellect, but he's an excellent, spontaneous thinker, a keen-witted athlete with a unique field of vision. And he will not choke," Walsh said.

Montana became Walsh's special project. Montana fit in perfectly with Walsh's newfangled system, the West Coast Offense, which emphasized timing routes and precise passes to specific places on the field. Walsh's offense was complicated, and he was careful not to ruin the confidence of his young quarterback. He used Montana selectively during his rookie year and the beginning of his second year. "We didn't want to throw him to the wolves," Walsh said. "We thought it was important to give him moments of success early to build his confidence."

Montana became the regular starter midway through his second year. He played well, but it was only a prelude to brilliance. In 1981, the 49ers were a vastly improved team. They went from 2-14 in 1979 to 6-10 in 1980 before breaking out in a big way in '81. They got on a roll, Montana leading the way. The 49ers were an NFL-best 13-3 in 1981.

The NFC title game was a classic—the 49ers against the Dallas Cowboys in a game that featured six lead changes. Montana settled things with a touchdown pass to Dwight Clark with 51 seconds remaining in the fourth quarter. Flushed right, Montana at the last second before going out of bounds threw the ball high to the back of the end zone. Was he throwing the ball away? No. Out of nowhere, Clark suddenly appeared, leaping above star Dallas cornerback Everson Walls to complete the play—a legendary one dubbed "The Catch." It gave the 49ers a 26–21 victory that sent them into the Super Bowl for the first time. Their opponents: the Cincinnati Bengals, also there for the first time.

Played in the Silverdome in Pontiac, Michigan, Super Bowl XVI echoed the excitement of the NFC title game. The Bengals lost two fumbles and an interception, turnovers that helped the 49ers take a 20–0 lead at halftime. The Bengals were undaunted, climbing back behind quarterback Ken Anderson to cut the 49ers' lead to 20–7 in the third quarter. Two possessions later, the 49ers essentially decided the contest with a tremendous goal-line stand. The Bengals had moved to the 49ers' 3 yard line with a first-and-goal. On fourth-and-1, Anderson handed off to 249-pound fullback Peter Johnson. He was stopped cold. "It was the first time all year that we were stopped on that play," Bengals coach Forrest Gregg

Dan Ross

He came from a small town, Everett, Massachusetts. He played small college ball at Northeastern. But he had big dreams of being a Super Bowl hero. Dan Ross's dreams came true, even if in defeat. Northeastern, in Boston, never has been recognized for its football program. The big schools weren't exactly knocking down Ross's doors, though, and Ross liked staying close to home. So how do you get from Northeastern to the pros? Work your butt off. When he was chosen 30th in the NFL's 1979 draft by the Cincinnati Bengals, he was on his way.

The Bengals made their way to Super Bowl XVI to face the San Francisco 49ers and Ross was ecstatic. Nervous, too. Very nervous. "I've been nervous, but never like this," Ross said. "You can talk all you want during the week about this just being another football game, but it isn't."

Ross had stage fright. He thought his whole team had it, too, for the first half of the game. He knew people all over the world were watching on television.

The first half was a flop for the Bengals. They turned over the ball three times, allowing the 49ers to take a 20–0 lead.

In the locker room at halftime, Bengals coach Forrest Gregg encouraged his players. "If we went out in the second half and did [play our game], we could still win," Ross said.

A key sequence came late in the third period. With the Niners leading 20–7, the Bengals had the ball on the 1 yard line but failed to get it into the end zone on three tries.

"We didn't make it there, and that devastated us," Ross said.

Yet the Bengals were still in the game with Ross's help. In the fourth quarter, Ross scored twice on touchdown passes from Ken Anderson. Too late. The 49ers held on to win, 26–21.

Ross surpassed the record of eight catches set by George Sauer of the New York Jets in Super Bowl III. Ross actually did more than his share. He caught a record-setting 11 passes for 104 yards in one of the greatest individual performances in Super Bowl history.

It wasn't satisfying enough for Ross. "I would give back every catch, everything that I did in the game," Ross said, "if we could win instead."

said. Amazingly, the 49ers managed to stuff Johnson despite using only 10 defenders. The Bengals eventually cut the 49ers' lead to five points, but the 49ers held on.

Montana was voted Super Bowl MVP after completing 14 of 22 passes for 157 yards, scoring one touchdown on a quarterback sneak, and passing for another.

Montana had learned his lessons well in the incubator of Walsh's West Coast Offense.

"The critical thing with Joe is his natural instinct for sports and competitiveness," Walsh said. "Joe has that one great asset that so many other athletes don't—his instincts.

"A mechanical athlete, one who has been programmed, sometimes loses his effectiveness in big games because that is where he loses his confidence. But that is when Joe is at his best."

Super Bowl XVII

ONE YEAR, JOHN RIGGINS WAS SITTING ON A FARM IN KANSAS LISTENing to the cows in the distance. Two years later, he was listening to the roar of the crowd at Super Bowl XVII. "I never had any idea I would be playing in a Super Bowl and be on a championship team," Riggins said.

Riggins sat out the 1980 season because the Washington Redskins wouldn't guarantee the last year of his contract. When he came back, Riggins was asked if he got a new perspective from his year off.

"Yes," the big fullback responded, "through the eyes of a banker."

Sitting out the year was a gutsy thing to do. Many thought Riggins would never get back, but Riggins never did the ordinary. He followed his own beat, a true maverick.

He loved shocking people. He wore an Afro before it was fashionable, then a Mohawk, and even had his head shaved.

At a media session during Super Bowl week, Riggins showed up wearing army camouflage pants with an elephant gun belt buckle. Then Riggins wowed a packed ballroom by grabbing the mike and holding an individual press conference before the entire house.

Nothing traditional for Riggins. Later in the week, he got a standing ovation when he showed up in white tie, top hat, and tails at a party hosted by Redskins owner Jack Kent Cooke.

He was no less spectacular in the playoffs.

After the Redskins made the postseason, Riggins approached coach Joe Gibbs with some advice.

"I went to Gibbs and said, 'Joe, let me tell you how to win this thing. Give me the ball.'"

Gibbs took Riggins's advice. In three playoff games, all won easily by the Redskins, Riggins churned out 25, 37, and 36 carries, with the yardage well above 100 in each game.

The 1982–83 season was difficult for the National Football League with a players' strike that significantly shortened the schedule to nine games. The bitterness of the strike was in everybody's memory. It was also the year Al Davis won a court battle, moving his Raiders from Oakland to Los Angeles. Riggins was a delightful distraction after such turmoil. Super Bowl XVII at the Rose Bowl was his time to soar.

One of the largest crowds in Super Bowl history eagerly awaited a classic battle between the Redskins and Miami Dolphins. It was a matchup between the top two defenses in the league, with the Dolphins ranked No. 1. Asked who Riggins reminded him of, Miami coach Don Shula immediately responded: Larry Csonka.

Like Riggins, Csonka loved to play smash-mouth football, a powerful fullback with strength enough to knock over opponents. Csonka had led the Dolphins to two Super Bowl titles in the early 1970s.

The Dolphins knew they had to stop Riggins or else their experience in Pasadena would hardly be filled with roses. And early in the game, it seemed they would be successful.

The first half was highlighted by a game-record 98-yard kickoff return by the Dolphins' Fulton Walker just before the end of the first half. The only kickoff ever returned all the way in a Super Bowl to that point gave the Dolphins a 17–10 halftime lead.

Then Riggins, operating behind Washington's "Hogs," took over.

The Hogs was a term coined by offensive line coach Joe Bugel during the Redskins' training camp in 1982. During a drill, Bugel shouted to Russ Grimm and Jeff Bostic, "Okay, you hogs, let's get running down there." Along with left guard Grimm and center Bostic, the Hogs featured right guard Mark May, left tackle Joe Jacoby, right tackle George Starke, and tight ends Don Warren and Rick Walker. The line averaged 273 pounds in 1982.

The Hogs were responsible for one of the most powerful running games in the NFL. "Riggo" was accepted into the Hogs fraternity as an

"Honorary Hog," an honor that escaped quarterback Joe Theismann. The Hogs refused to accept Theismann as an honorary member because he never had to hit a blocking dummy in practice. After a while, though, Theismann was accepted by his teammates as a "Piglet."

Theismann did save the Redskins from potential defeat in this Super Bowl, however. The Dolphins were leading 17–13 late in the third quarter with the ball on Washington's 18 yard line. Theismann went to the air, but the ball was tipped by defensive end Kim Bokamper.

As Bokamper settled under the ball at the goal line, waiting for it to come down for a sure interception, Theismann came out of nowhere to knock away the ball. That saved the Redskins from allowing a probable score and clincher for the Dolphins.

It was Riggins—who else?—who soon drew the spotlight and would seal the Redskins' first NFL title since 1942 with one of the best runs of his career.

Down by that same 17–13 score and with the ball on the Miami 43, it was fourth-and-1. The Redskins had a choice: go for the first down or punt and put the Dolphins deep in their own territory.

Go for it, the Redskins decided. Why not, with Riggo in the backfield? The call: 70-Chip out of the I-Formation. "It's a play we ran all season," Riggins said.

Riggins took the handoff from Theismann and cut to his left, straight-arming Miami cornerback Don McNeal, who grabbed Riggins high on his white number 44 jersey. No luck. He slid down the fullback's legs and was left sprawling on the turf.

Riggins raced down the left sideline to complete a 43-yard touchdown run. There were 10 minutes left, and Riggins's go-ahead run would be decisive. It was the longest TD run in any of the first 17 Super Bowls.

With two minutes left, Theismann threw a touchdown pass to Charlie Brown for the clincher. Washington 27, Miami 17.

Riggins had a field day, piling up 166 rushing yards to win the Super Bowl's MVP.

"I'm very happy," Riggins said, "but I'm very tired."

Super Bowl XVIII

MARCUS ALLEN WAS FRUSTRATED. THE HEISMAN TROPHY WINNER AND 1982 NFL Rookie of the Year felt he wasn't getting the ball often enough.

Most everyone was saying he was a disappointment during the 1983 season. Allen's figures were paltry compared to his 2,300-yard senior season at Southern Cal. He didn't cross the 1,000-yard mark until the final game of the year.

So he complained to Al Davis, the Raiders' owner. He wanted to carry the ball more.

Davis was not sympathetic. "We want to keep you fresh for the playoffs," Davis told Allen. "Our aim is to win games, not gain yards."

So Allen waited his turn. He shook off an early-season slump and when it came playoff time, Allen was playing his best. "We knew that all we had to do was give him a little bit of a hole and he'd do the rest himself," said Raiders tackle Bruce Davis.

Allen seemed to be preparing for this Super Bowl moment all his life.

Growing up in San Diego, Allen was recruited by Southern Cal as a defensive back. Trojans coach John Robinson switched Allen to the Trojans' famed tailback position, and Allen served as a backup to Heisman Trophy winner Charles White. As a starter, Allen blossomed into one of the nation's top backs, a versatile runner who was especially good in goal-line and short-yardage situations. Allen became the first college back to run for more than 2,000 yards in a season. He finished his senior year with 2,342 yards. In winning the Heisman, Allen was selected over a rich field that included Dan Marino, Herschel Walker, and Jim McMahon.

Allen was chosen in the first round of the NFL draft by the Los Angeles Raiders. His rookie year was sensational. Although the schedule was shortened by a strike, Allen rushed for 697 yards and scored a league-high 14 TDs to lead the Raiders to the best record in the AFC at 8-1. Allen was voted the *Sporting News* NFL Rookie of the Year. The Raiders weren't as successful as a team, losing to the New York Jets in the second round of the playoffs.

The next season was a different story. In the playoffs, Allen improved each week, gaining 121 yards in a 38–10 victory over the Pittsburgh Steelers, and 154 yards with three touchdowns in a 30–14 win in the AFC championship game against the Seattle Seahawks.

Next were the Washington Redskins in Super Bowl XVIII. As the defending league champions, the Redskins were winners of 11 games in a row and the NFL's highest-scoring team.

The talk all week in the Raiders' camp had been focused on the difficulty of stopping Redskins fullback John Riggins. In the Super Bowl the year before, Riggins had rushed for a record 166 yards and was voted MVP. Some thought it not possible to stop a man who had gained over 100 yards in six straight playoff games.

But what about the Raiders? They were so ready to play that in the Raiders' Wednesday practice there were near fights between players. They were that passionate about the game.

"We came in just wanting to win and break 100 yards rushing," Allen said. "A lot of teams have not done that against them." Although Allen started slowly, the Raiders took a 21–3 lead at the half. Then Allen showed what he could do.

The Redskins had driven 70 yards for a touchdown to cut the Raiders' lead to 21–9. Back came the Raiders midway through the third quarter on a 5-yard touchdown run by Allen to boost their lead to 28–9. Then came the clincher for Los Angeles, thanks to Allen's improvisational skills.

The Raiders had the ball on their 26 yard line when Allen took a handoff and swept to his left. There, he was met by a bunch of Washington players. He pulled up, reversed direction to his right. More company from defenders. Changing directions again, Allen burst toward the middle of the field past befuddled defenders. "I should have been inside, but I was outside," Allen said. "So I tried to make something out of nothing.

Jack Squirek

Jack Squirek, a minor player with the Los Angeles Raiders, was about to become a hero in Super Bowl XVIII because linebacker coach Charlie Sumner had a hunch.

The Washington Redskins were at their 12 yard line with only 12 seconds remaining in the first half. Los Angeles was ahead 14–3. There had been a similar situation in a 37–35 loss to Los Angeles earlier in the season.

"When they were backed up in that game," Sumner said, "they threw a screen pass to Joe Washington for 67 yards. I just knew it was coming again. That's why I wanted Squirek in there."

Matt Millen, a Raiders starting linebacker, protested. But Sumner insisted he needed Squirek in a prevent defense.

Joe Gibbs, the Redskins' coach, was looking at his options at the other side of the field. "We had two choices there," Gibbs said. "Fall on the ball or use a play that was safe."

Gibbs remembered the screen pass the Redskins had used against the Raiders earlier in the season and considered it safe. Let's try to get it upfield, Gibbs told his quarterback, Joe Theismann. "Use the rocket right, screen left," he said.

That was the play that Charlie Sumner remembered.

At the snap, Theismann drifted back and passed to running back Joe Washington. "The defensive end had grabbed Joe by the shirt," Theismann said, "and the linebacker had him man to man."

Theismann thought Joe Washington would be open. Instead, Squirek was ready, thanks to his coach's hunch. Squirek moved in front of the Redskins' Washington, picked off the pass, and ran untouched into the end zone.

The Raiders took a 21–3 lead into the dressing room. They were on their way to a 38–9 victory over the Redskins, the biggest blowout in Super Bowl history at the time.

Squirek, a second-year reserve linebacker from Illinois, had his 15 minutes of fame.

Luckily I saw a few holes and I broke up the middle, and Cliff Branch came through with a block."

Allen completed a 74-yard TD dash. At the time, it was the longest run from scrimmage in Super Bowl history. It gave the Raiders a 35–9 advantage and clinched the MVP trophy for Allen. The Raiders added a field goal to make the final score 38–9.

"They said I couldn't go the distance," Allen said, "and I guess I proved them wrong."

Super Bowl XIX

In his first Super Bowl appearance, San Francisco's Roger Craig scored a touchdown. Turns out he was only getting started.

In short order, Craig added his second and third TDs in one of the greatest offensive performances in Super Bowl history. The scores came at such a dizzying speed that Craig's breakout game stunned the crowd at Palo Alto, California, not to mention the Miami Dolphins.

After the 38–16 rout of the Dolphins by the 49ers in Super Bowl XIX, Craig stood uncertain in the locker room. He was trying to recall a key play, the 16-yard touchdown reception that sealed the game for San Francisco.

Craig remembered that the play was changed at the line of scrimmage by Joe Montana. The 49ers quarterback had called an audible so he could put Craig into scoring position. When Craig crossed the goal line, it capped a day in which he also scored on an 8-yard TD pass and a 2-yard touchdown run. Craig was in such a state of euphoria that it was hard for him to differentiate between his touchdowns.

"Was that the second or the third?" Craig said in response to a reporter's question about the 16-yard run. "I don't even know. I just remember going over the goal line."

It was that kind of day for Craig, exhausted after setting a Super Bowl record with his splendid performance.

"At Nebraska, they never really passed that much to the backs, or passed anywhere," Craig said. With the Cornhuskers, he was a Heisman hopeful until he was switched from tailback to fullback. Coach Tom Osborne wanted to groom Mike Rozier for the Heisman.

"I could have said, 'No, I don't want to play fullback,'" Craig said. "I was a candidate for the Heisman. A lot of people said, 'Are you crazy?'"

As a junior tailback, Craig had gained over 1,000 yards and Nebraska's media guide featured him on the cover. As a fullback, he knew that he wouldn't get the yardage to compete with other Heisman candidates.

But Craig is easygoing and wanted to be the best all-around player he could be. He became a fullback and got lots of experience blocking.

Still, the scouting report on Craig wasn't that enthusiastic. Running upright made him too large a target, the report said, and he had a reputation as a fumbler. However, "he had excellent speed and moves."

San Francisco coach Bill Walsh wasn't deterred by any of the negativity. He felt Craig would fit into his program, so the 49ers made Craig their first pick in the draft. Walsh was sure he could use him as a receiver as well as a running back.

In Super Bowl XIX, Craig didn't disappoint. He was one of Montana's favorite targets.

All the talk in the week leading up to the big game revolved around Miami's Dan Marino, one of the NFL's top passers. "No one gave our defense any credit, either," said Montana. "All they'd heard was how you couldn't stop Marino, or [receivers Mark] Clayton and [Mark] Duper. Our whole team had something to prove."

And prove it they did. In the middle of it were Craig and Montana. "There were only one or two pass plays in the whole ballgame where Roger was the primary receiver," said Paul Hackett, the quarterbacks coach at Craig's first 49ers minicamp. But Craig made the most of his opportunities.

Craig's first score came on the 8-yard pass from Montana. He slipped past Dolphins linebacker Jay Brophy to give the 49ers a 14–10 lead. The touchdown capped a 47-yard drive early in the second quarter.

Craig's second TD, on a running play called "11 Leap," came at the end of a 52-yard drive and gave San Francisco a 28–10 lead. The running back scored his last touchdown of the game on that 16-yard run off Montana's audible.

The secondary receiver was Craig. He ran right to left across the field and caught the pass. He used his "excellent speed" mentioned in the scouting report and headed untouched toward the end zone.

"I was just hoping some of the calls would come to me," Craig said. And they did. In record fashion. Craig ran for 58 yards and one touchdown and caught seven passes for 77 yards and two touchdowns.

Montana, meanwhile, set a Super Bowl record with 331 passing yards. He completed 24 of 35 passes, threw for three touchdowns, and when he couldn't find a receiver, he even rushed for 59 yards on five carries. He was voted the game's Most Valuable Player.

"Montana was outstanding in every way," Dolphins coach Don Shula said. "Every time we tried to put pressure on him, he scrambled for a big play on his own or he bought time to hit one of his receivers."

The 49ers' defense, meanwhile, did a great job stifling Marino and company. "The 49er defensive schemes nearly eliminated Miami's running game," the *New York Times* reported.

Incredibly, the 49ers' defense held the Dolphins to only 25 yards on the ground. The Dolphins played mostly a passing game, and Marino completed 29 of 50 passes, both records, for 318 yards. But he only threw one touchdown pass, a 2-yarder, and was sacked four times, more than in any other game of the season.

Afterward in the raucous 49ers locker room, Craig was wearing his new T-shirt. Across the front it read, "World Champion 49ers." No one could argue with that.

Super Bowl XX

THE SCOREBOARD READ: CHICAGO BEARS 46, NEW ENGLAND PATRIOTS 10. Just call them "Monsters of the Midway," the sequel.

Sounds like a horror film, and it was indeed horrifying for opposing teams to face the Chicago Bears in the 1980s. Like their famed predecessors of the 1940s, the 1985 Bears were a fearsome and formidable group. The cast included Richard "Sack Master" Dent, Walter "Sweetness" Payton, William "The Refrigerator" Perry, and Jim "Rebel" McMahon.

Add in a splendid supporting cast, all under the direction of Mike Ditka, Da Coach of Da Bears.

Da Bears—characters all.

"They captured the imagination of everyone," said the always colorful Ditka. "One reason was, I never reined them in. I let them go. I let their personalities show. I let their characters show."

Ditka, a three-sport athlete at Pitt, was an All-Pro tight end with the Bears before taking over as coach from 1982 to 1992 and enjoying a good deal of success. "I believe everyone has a destiny in life, and mine is with the Chicago Bears," Ditka said.

William Perry, also known as "The Fridge," had his comic side. He was a 308-pound defensive lineman sometimes used on offense. One time during a game, Perry picked up a surprised Payton and tossed him over the line into the end zone for a touchdown. Of course, it was illegal.

In his last game in college, Richard Dent played with a broken arm to impress his mom. He wanted to break the school record of three sacks. He got four sacks and eight tackles. "I had to give my mom a good performance," he said. An eighth-round draft pick from Tennessee State, he ended up as the Bears' career sack leader with 137½ as a four-time Pro Bowler.

This unforgettable cast did its work in two acts.

ACT I—THE REGULAR SEASON

This zany group was cocky and confident as it marched through opponents in 1985. With three weeks to go in the regular season, the players decided to make a music video. Called the "Super Bowl Shuffle," 10 of the Bears sang and danced—what, you've never seen a dancing or singing Bear? They taped the session after their first (and only) loss to the Miami Dolphins. They were such an arrogant bunch they hadn't considered losing.

"I thought, 'We better win the Super Bowl now, or we'll look like a bunch of jerks,'" said center Jay Hilgenberg.

Perry became the center of attention in a game against the San Francisco 49ers. The previous year, the 49ers had beaten the Bears. Ditka decided to use 308-pound Perry on offense. It surprised everyone; how often did anyone see 300-pounders in the offensive backfield?

"I just wanted to see if Perry could run with it," said Ditka. He could, at least from short range, scoring two touchdowns during the regular season as the Bears finished with a 15-1 record.

ACT II—THE PLAYOFFS/SUPER BOWL XX

Going into the playoffs, Ditka advised his team to remain arrogant. Always carry a chip on their shoulders and dare opponents to knock it off. The arrogance worked.

The Bears smothered the Giants (21–0) and the Rams (24–0) on the way to the Super Bowl. "We didn't allow you to think you could play with us, we didn't allow you second chances. We would finish you from the get-go," Dent said.

And, from the get-go, during Super Bowl week in New Orleans, the Bears and the fans enjoyed the raucous activities on Bourbon Street. After curfew. Headlines? You bet!

When a helicopter hovered over the Bears' field one practice day, McMahon, the high-spirited, flamboyant quarterback, mooned the copter. Headlines? You bet!

The Big Bad Bears were in town.

"I was on my regular routine—having some fun," McMahon said.

McMahon already had enjoyed some costly fun.

In the NFC divisional playoff against the Giants, McMahon wore a headband with the name of a sporting goods company, Adidas.

NFL commissioner Pete Rozelle fined McMahon $5,000.

The next game, McMahon wore a headband with the name of the commissioner on it. Around his neck was an Adidas headband.

Always a maverick, during the Super Bowl, McMahon wore three different headbands: JDF Cure (Juvenile Diabetes Foundation), POW-MIA (a reference to missing-in-action or prisoner-of-war military members in the Vietnam War), and Pluto (college friend battling cancer).

The Bears were 10-point favorites in Super Bowl XX, but the beginning was not favorable. Payton, whose nickname was attributed to his sweet running style, fumbled on the second play, and New England recovered on the Chicago 19. The Patriots scored the quickest points in Super Bowl history as Tony Franklin's field goal gave New England a 3–0 lead.

All that did was rile up the Bears. They scored the game's next 44 points.

Late in the first quarter, Ditka sent in Refrigerator Perry to attempt a pass. This was before a potential television audience of 100 million–plus and 73,818 in the Superdome. The Fridge was sacked.

But Perry redeemed himself by scoring a touchdown later in the game, which irked many purists because Payton didn't get into the end zone in his only Super Bowl.

The Bears' defense led by Dent held New England to 7 yards rushing and 116 yards passing. Dent, voted the game's Most Valuable Player, had a hand in two sacks and forced two fumbles early in the game.

The final score: Bears 46, Patriots 10. "We were going for 60, but we ran out of time," said McMahon.

Da Bears were on their way to a celebration. Look out, Bourbon Street.

Super Bowl XXI

FROM ZERO TO HERO.

Phil Simms was on everyone's recruiting list as a high school quarterback. Then he injured his shoulder. He went to zero on recruiting lists. No football scholarship for Simms. It was typical of the way his football career would go.

There would be boos, jeers, and catcalls, enough to test the strongest of wills. There would be calls for him to be benched, even cut.

He went to little-known Morehead State and threw for 5,542 yards and 32 touchdowns with a run-oriented offense. It was enough to catch the attention of the New York Giants, who selected him as their No. 1 pick in the 1979 NFL draft.

When his name was announced at the draft, it started. Boos rang throughout the room—who was this guy? No one in New York had heard of him, and Giants fans couldn't understand why he was the team's first-round pick.

Over the next four seasons, 1980–1983, Simms suffered a variety of injuries that kept his performance below par: two shoulder separations, a knee injury, and a fractured thumb. A series of changes in coaches and players on the Giants didn't help. Fans were becoming discouraged and hostile, blaming the young quarterback. Simms understood, but he was shaken. "The quarterback of a bad team is going to look terrible," Simms said. "He's bound to be criticized, especially in New York."

The Giants went 6-10 in 1979 and 4-12 in 1980. Simms lost his starting job to Scott Brunner. He also lost his confidence and asked to be traded. Bill Parcells, the newly installed Giants coach, had something else in mind. "He sat me down and told me the kind of quarterback he wanted," Simms recalled of Parcells. "He was building a defense-oriented club, so we'd always have a lot of [good] field position. There'd be no need for me to force things."

In 1984, Parcells restored Simms to the starting quarterback's job and traded Brunner. Simms became the first in Giants history to pass for more than 4,000 yards. New York made the playoffs and upset the Rams in the first round before losing to San Francisco, the eventual Super Bowl winner. That still wasn't enough for Giants fans. They continued to boo Simms unmercifully, even though the Giants had started to turn things around with the help of Parcells and a huge-impact defensive star, linebacker Lawrence Taylor.

Then more trouble for Simms. In the first exhibition game of 1985, Simms came to the sidelines holding the small finger on his left hand. Pat Hodgson, the Giants' receivers coach, took a look at the finger. "I almost fainted," said Hodgson, who had joined the Giants in 1979 when Simms was a rookie and was witness to many of the quarterback's injuries. "I just said, 'Oh, no. Here it goes.'"

Simms felt the same way. It turned out to be a minor injury, but at the time, he showed his frustration. "I was really scared," he recalled. "I was beside myself. I said, 'If this damn finger is hurt, I'll quit. I'm not going to go through this any more.' I was panicky."

Obviously Simms didn't quit.

"Anytime an athlete gets injured, he's going to stick with it," Simms said. "So that's what I did."

Simms led the Giants to a 10-6 record in 1985 and won a first-round playoff game against the defending champion 49ers before the Giants were blanked by the powerhouse Bears.

The Giants entered the 1986 season as one of the favorites to win the Super Bowl. A key game during the season was against the Denver Broncos, a team they would meet in the Super Bowl. In that November 23, 1986, game, Simms felt the Broncos had not shown the Giants any respect. "They won the coin toss and kicked off to us, as if to tell us we couldn't move the ball on them," Simms said. The Giants squeezed out a 19–16 victory on their way to a 14-2 regular-season record.

A turning point of the season, according to Simms, was a December 1 game against the 49ers. The Giants trailed by 17 points at the half when coach Parcells directed his remarks to Simms. "He said we had to become more aggressive passing the ball. 'Get it up the field. Head north. Quit worrying about what might go wrong,'" Simms recalled.

Simms took it to heart. "He got through to me," Simms said. "We beat the 49ers in the second half and we kept it going."

In the playoffs, the Giants routed San Francisco 49–3 and blanked Washington 17–0 in a bitterly cold wind before meeting Denver in Super Bowl XXI at the Rose Bowl.

Once again, even though the Giants were favorites, media attention was centered on league MVP Lawrence Taylor and opposing quarterback John Elway. "I really didn't mind," Simms said. "John's a great player. And it took the pressure off of me."

In the Giants' camp, Parcells and his coaches made a radical decision before the game. They knew the Broncos were expecting a running game sparked by Joe Morris, one of the league's top rushers. They changed tactics.

"I knew we were going to start out being aggressive, trying to throw the ball," Simms said. "I didn't want to run, run, get to third-and-10 and ask me to get 10 yards, do it again and get 8, then wonder why we're not in the game in the first quarter. I wanted a chance to be a factor in the game." This was his chance of a lifetime. "All I knew was that my whole career was riding on the game," Simms said.

Talk about pressure. With over 101,063 fans in attendance, millions more watching on TV, the Giants reeled off 11 first downs in the first half and Simms threw for nine of them, including a touchdown pass. Simms completed 12 of 15 passes for 103 yards by intermission. Yet the Giants went into the tunnel trailing 10–9.

Parcells was not concerned. He was expecting a close game. He told his players not to worry because they were moving the ball without much trouble against the Broncos' defense.

The Giants came out with a purpose in the second half. Simms had been feeling good all week about this game, and now was about to truly step up. Simms thought the game's turning point came early in the second half when the Giants lined up in punt formation on fourth-and-1 on their 46 yard line. The punt never came. All of a sudden, the Giants went into an offensive formation. Jeff Rutledge took the snap for a quarterback sneak for two yards and a first down.

Back on the field, Simms moved the Giants downfield for a touchdown and a 16–10 lead. The Giants romped from there. By using that play, with his team behind and the Super Bowl at stake, Parcells showed his faith in his players. They didn't let him down.

"This game is not for faint-hearted people," Parcells said. Simms proved he was not faint-hearted, either. In his greatest performance, a Super Bowl record-breaker no less, Simms was nearly perfect. He completed 22 of 25 passes as the Giants walloped the Broncos, 39–20. Simms was selected the game's MVP. The jeers had turned to cheers.

Super Bowl XXII

IT ONLY TOOK A MOMENT IN TIME. TIMMY SMITH HAD ONE OF THOSE unforgettable games. This one just happened to be in the Super Bowl.

An obscure rookie running back for the Washington Redskins, Smith didn't expect to play in Super Bowl XXII. He got a surprising start and rushed his way into the record book.

Smith gained 204 yards—breaking Marcus Allen's single-game Super Bowl mark of 191—on 22 carries and scored two touchdowns. Washington routed Denver 42–10.

George Rogers was the regular running back for the Redskins and was ready to play. Until coach Joe Gibbs had a talk with Rogers.

"I decided Saturday night to start Timmy Smith at running back. I knew George Rogers, our usual starter, was gimpy all week," Gibbs said. "I told him I wanted to start Timmy the first few plays."

The coaches were keeping the decision to start a secret from Smith. "We didn't tell Timmy anything, because we didn't want him getting sick in our locker room," said offensive coordinator Joe Bugel.

To keep up the charade, Rogers was introduced Super Bowl morning as the starter.

Smith's journey to the top of the football world was uneven at best. He led the Texas Tech Red Raiders in rushing for two years, and then sat out his junior and senior seasons with injuries. In his senior year trying for a comeback, Smith ran for a touchdown. Holding the ball up in a showy manner for all to see, Smith was blindsided by an angry New Mexico State player. The jarring collision wrecked Smith's knee.

Surprisingly, the Redskins made him the 117th pick in the 1987 draft. Then on January 31, 1988, a star was born. And just as quickly as his meteoric rise, he disappeared. The Redskins let him go the following year and he spent a short time with Dallas before his NFL career ended.

Smith's personal life didn't go well, either. In 2006, he was imprisoned for distributing cocaine. Upon his release from prison, he became a bus dispatcher.

He never parlayed his Super Bowl outing into anything memorable. But he had his moment in the biggest of sports spotlights. "That's the beauty of it: One great play, one big moment in a big game, and you become a household name," Allen said. "Tim Smith rushed for more than 200 yards and we never really heard from him again. But the biggest game, the biggest stage—he performed."

January 20, 1980; Pasadena,CA, USA; Pittsburgh Steelers quarterback Terry Brad-
shaw (12) in action against the Los Angeles Rams during Super Bowl XIV at the
Rose Bowl. Bradshaw received his second consecutive Super Bowl MVP award.
Pittsburgh defeated Los Angeles 31-19 to earn its fourth Super Bowl championship
and its second back-to-back championship. PHOTO BY MALCOLM EMMONS-USA TODAY
SPORTS COPYRIGHT 1979 MALCOLM EMMONS

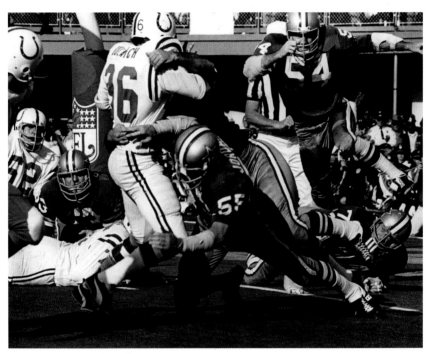

January 17, 1971; Miami, FL, USA; FILE PHOTO; Baltimore Colts running back
Norm Bulaich (36) is stopped by Dallas Cowboys linebacker Leroy Jordan (55) and
Chuck Howley (54) during Super Bowl V at the Orange Bowl. The Colts defeated
the Cowboys 16-13 to earn their first Super Bowl title. PHOTO BY MALCOLM EMMONS-
USA TODAY SPORTS COPYRIGHT MALCOLM EMMONS

January 20, 1980; Pasadena, CA, USA; FILE PHOTO; Pittsburgh Steelers receiver John Stallworth (82) catches a 73-yard touchdown pass in the fourth quarter past Los Angeles Rams defensive back Rod Perry (49) during Super Bowl XIV at the Rose Bowl. The Steelers defeated the Rams 31-19. DARRYL NORENBERG-USA TODAY SPORTS

January 13, 1974; Houston, TX, USA; FILE PHOTO; Miami Dolphins running back Larry Csonka in action against the Minnesota Vikings during Super Bowl VIII at Rice Stadium. Miami defeated Minnesota 24-7. DICK RAPHAEL-USA TODAY SPORTS

January 25, 1998; San Diego, CA, USA; FILE PHOTO; Denver Broncos quarter-back John Elway in action against the Green Bay Packers during Super Bowl XXXII at Qualcomm Stadium. The Broncos defeated the Packers 31-24. RVR PHOTOS-USA TODAY SPORTS

January 30, 1983; Pasadena, CA, USA; FILE PHOTO; Washington Redskins running back John Riggins breaks free on a 43-yard touchdown run against the Miami Dolphins during Super Bowl XVII at the Rose Bowl. Riggins was named the game's Most Valuable Player as he rushed for 166 yards on 38 carries and a touchdown. The Redskins defeated the Dolphins 27-17. TONY TOMSIC-USA TODAY SPORT

January 31, 1988; San Diego, CA, USA; FILE PHOTO; Washington Redskins quarterback Doug Williams looks to throw against the Denver Broncos during Super Bowl XXII at Jack Murphy Stadium. Washington defeated Denver 42-10. MANNY RUBIO-USA TODAY SPORTS

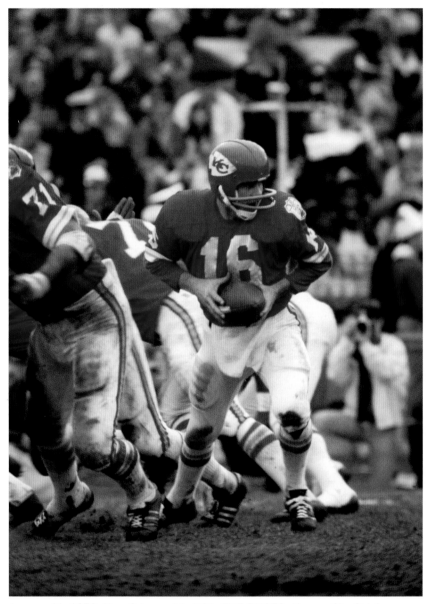

January 11, 1970; New Orleans, LA, USA; FILE PHOTO; Kansas City Chiefs quarterback Len Dawson in action against the Minnesota Vikings in Super Bowl IV at Tulane Stadium. The Chiefs defeated the Vikings 23-7. PHOTO BY MALCOLM EMMONS-USA TODAY SPORTS COPYRIGHT MALCOLM EMMONS

January 12, 1969; Miami, FL, USA; FILE PHOTO; New York Jets quarterback Joe Namath on the sidelines against the Baltimore Colts in Super Bowl III at the Orange Bowl. Namath was the game's Most Valuable Player as the Jets defeated the Colts 16-7 to win the first-ever Super Bowl title for the AFL. PHOTO BY MALCOLM EMMONS-USA TODAY SPORTS COPYRIGHT MALCOLM EMMONS

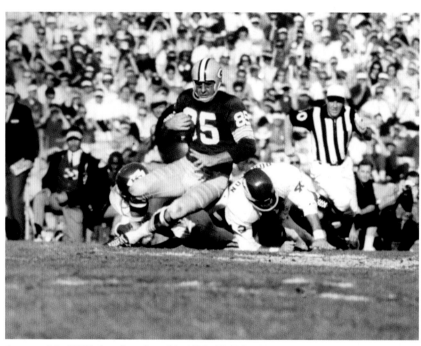

January 15, 1967; Los Angeles, CA, USA; FILE PHOTO; Green Bay Packers receiver Max McGee (85) in action during Super Bowl I against the Kansas City Chiefs at the Los Angeles Memorial Coliseum. The Packers defeated the Chiefs 35-10. DARRYL NORENBERG-USA TODAY SPORTS

February 1, 2015; Glendale, AZ, USA; New England Patriots defensive back Malcolm Butler (21) intercepts a pass intended for Seattle Seahawks wide receiver Ricardo Lockette (83) in the fourth quarter in Super Bowl XLIX at University of Phoenix Stadium. MARK J. REBILAS-USA TODAY SPORTS

February 1, 2015; Glendale, AZ, USA; Detailed view of a banner of Seattle Seahawks quarterback Russell Wilson (right) and New England Patriots quarterback Tom Brady during Super Bowl XLIX at University of Phoenix Stadium.

Super Bowl XXIII-XXIV

.

A SUPER PERFORMANCE BY JERRY RICE. AND ANOTHER BY JOE MONTANA.

Sure, you can always count on Super Bowls bringing out the very best in players. But few ever matched the performances of Rice and Montana in consecutive championship games when they were playing for the San Francisco 49ers in the 80s.

In Super Bowl XXIII, Rice had an 11-catch day for 215 yards as the 49ers beat the Cincinnati Bengals 20–16. In Super Bowl XXIV, one year later, San Francisco beat Denver 55–10 with Montana playing a key role and outplaying John Elway by a wide margin.

Major Super Bowl records were set in those two games. Rice's 11 catches tied a Super Bowl record and his 215-yard total set a new mark in San Francisco's comeback win over the Bengals. The 49ers also set another standard in beating Denver: The 45-point margin of victory was the largest in Super Bowl history. Call that one a Big Easy in the Big Easy.

No surprise, Rice was selected as the MVP in Super Bowl XXIII and Montana in Super Bowl XXIV.

Rice had a habit of destroying opponents in a big way, and he set some receiving records that might never be surpassed: most notably, the career mark for touchdowns once held by Cleveland's Jim Brown, merely the greatest running back the pro game has seen. And Rice did it in style.

Brown had scored 126 TDs in his record-breaking career with the Browns. Rice came into the 1994 season needing two touchdowns to tie Brown and another one to surpass him.

What better place to do it than on *Monday Night Football*, when the entire pro football world was watching Rice's 49ers face the Los Angeles Raiders? He didn't waste any time. Rice scored a touchdown, then scored

.

another to lead the 49ers to a 37–14 blowout lead late in the game. Rice's second touchdown of the night was scored on a 23-yard reverse play with 12:15 to play.

Rice needed one more TD to break Brown's record. But with his team holding a 23-point lead late in the game, Rice thought he was done for the night. Although there are exceptions when personal revenge is in order, usually pro football teams don't try to embarrass opponents, especially on a big stage like *Monday Night Football* before a crowd of 68,032 in San Francisco and a national TV audience of millions.

"We're sitting on the bench and thinking, 'OK, it's not going to happen here,'" Rice recalled of his attempt to pass Brown's touchdown record. "'Maybe next ballgame.' And then [49ers coach George] Seifert walks down the bench and says, 'I'm going to give you a chance to do it tonight.'"

Naturally, Rice responded, taking advantage of the opportunity by catching a touchdown pass from Steve Young. Touchdown number 127 was in the books for Rice.

What makes an extraordinary receiver such as Rice?

He grew up in the South, the son of a bricklayer. He developed strong, calloused hands helping his dad. Rice always had a hankering to run, and on the rural roads of Mississippi, he would run miles and miles to meet friends, then run back home. No matter the weather, Rice would run.

"I don't know why," he said then. "It was not like I thought I was going to make it to the pros, or anything. For some reason I had to go out there and train hard."

He lived in a rural area, where the big city was Starkville, 38 miles down the highway. In a meadow near his house, horses were grazing. "If you wanted to ride, you chased them down," Rice said. "And then you rode them bareback."

This developed Rice's speed and agility. And he needed strong hands to hold on to the horse.

Growing up, Rice's football hero was Lynn Swann, the acrobatic receiver of the Pittsburgh Steelers. Rice liked Swann's elegant, acrobatic style. "He would amaze me," said Rice, "how he'd fly through the air and come up with big catches."

In high school, Rice was a pass-catching machine, catching the attention of Mississippi Valley State, the only school to recruit him. There, Rice helped put them on the football map.

In one fantastic game, Rice caught 24 passes and had four others called back by penalties. He hauled in more than 100 passes in each of his last two seasons, facing constant double-teaming. The accomplishments earned Rice a spot on the Little All-America team.

At the 1985 NFL draft, Rice was hopeful of being the first receiver picked, but his disappointment grew as two receivers, Al Toon to the Jets and Eddie Brown to the Bengals, came off the board. Seeing an opportunity to grab what the 49ers considered the best wideout in the class, coach Bill Walsh made a deal with New England to move up from 28th. The 49ers, who had already won two Super Bowls with Montana, made Rice the No. 16 pick.

Adjusting to NFL life was tough for Rice coming out of a small town. His performance on the field was unreliable. He would catch some passes and drop many others. He was booed by fans in Candlestick Park early in his rookie season whenever he dropped the ball.

"He needed to relax," Montana said. "He just needed to relax." He did. And soon, no defensive back could relax while covering Rice.

Rice soon made everyone believers, especially after one game in December when he made 10 catches for 241 yards against the Los Angeles Rams.

Rice was voted the 1985 NFC Offensive Rookie of the Year after making 49 catches for 927 yards, an average of 18.9 per catch. But it didn't translate to team success as the 49ers were knocked out of the playoffs in each of Rice's first three seasons.

Then came 1988, when Rice had his breakout game in Super Bowl XXIII.

Before the game against the Cincinnati Bengals, the 49ers were concerned about an injury to Rice's ankle. "I was a little scared [earlier in the week] about it," Rice said. "But in a situation like this there was no way I was going to sit out." Rice expected the Bengals to play him man to man, as they had all year against other great receivers. "I knew they weren't going to change for this game," Rice said. "I felt I could exploit that defense."

Montana felt the same way. "You can't play man to man against Rice and get away with it very long."

With only seconds left in the first quarter, Rice made one of his signature plays. Passing into a swirling wind, Montana tossed the ball toward Rice on the sideline.

Just as the ball appeared to be headed out of bounds, Rice snatched it and brought it back in. Result: a 15-yard gain.

With 11:05 left in the fourth quarter, Rice went deep to snare a high pass from Montana. Bengals defender Lewis Billups was shadowing Rice stride for stride. Reminiscent of his hero, Swann, Rice leaped into the air with Billups trying to bring him down. Rice caught the ball and then got slammed by the Bengals defender. But Rice managed to hold onto the ball for a 44-yard gain.

"When you're up in the air, you're not thinking about who's around you," Rice said. "When you're coming down, all you're thinking of is holding onto the ball."

As spectacular as those catches were, neither contributed to a touchdown. In the fourth quarter with the game on the line, Rice made his most spectacular contribution.

The 49ers trailed the Bengals 16–13 with 3:20 to play. Del Rodgers returned a kickoff, but a penalty put the 49ers back at their 8 yard line. They had to go 92 yards to win. Rice remembers looking down that field and thinking the goal line looked so far away.

"Some of the guys seemed more than normally tense," Montana recalled. Montana was known as "Mr. Cool" by his teammates. As Montana was assessing the situation, he happened to spot the late actor John Candy in the stands. "Look," Montana said. "Isn't that John Candy?" Unexpected, with the Super Bowl on the line, it did what Montana expected—it broke the tension. "Everybody kind of smiled, and then we all concentrated on the job we had to do," Montana said.

Some of the Bengals believed the game was over and said so. Not wide receiver Cris Collinsworth. Collinsworth asked "Is No. 16 in the huddle?" referring to Montana. "Yeah," replied his teammate. "It ain't over."

Everyone was expecting Montana to throw to Rice, who he looked for even when Rice was triple-teamed. Rice somehow eluded the triple team and took off running with rookie Rickey Dixon in pursuit.

Rice was finally pulled down by Dixon after a 27-yard gain. That set up Montana's TD pass to John Taylor from 10 yards out in the final moments, giving the 49ers a 20–16 victory in one of the most exciting Super Bowl endings.

Rice's MVP trophy marked only the third time in NFL history it was given to a receiver. His reaction upon learning he was selected? "If it was up to me, I would have given the MVP to Joe."

Montana didn't have to wait long to pick up another Super Bowl MVP. That occurred the very next season as the 49ers won their second straight league title. Winning Super Bowl MVPs had become a habit for Montana, who won the award for the third time in Super Bowl XXIV.

Montana endured his share of adversity to reach the top of his profession. At Notre Dame, he suffered a variety of injuries and missed his entire junior season with a broken collarbone. He was redshirted and didn't start a full season at Notre Dame until his fifth year.

Montana had the ability to inspire his teammates. He was especially good in desperate situations late in the game. His teammates believed that no matter what the score was, if Joe was on the field everything would turn out right. And it generally did.

When the 49ers made Montana a third-round draft pick in 1979, there were questions about the strength of his arm. Three quarterbacks were selected ahead of Montana in the NFL draft, all taken in the first round. "We thought he was a third- or fourth-round pick who would have a chance, in the right system, to maybe be a starter," said Chiefs general manager Carl Peterson, "but probably more like a good, steady backup."

If Montana had not played in Bill Walsh's system, he almost certainly would not have been as successful. "There's no coach I could have played for who would have been better for my career," Montana said. "Absolutely none."

Montana was always fighting to stay on top. Greatness didn't come easy for the legendary quarterback. Throughout his career in both college and the pros, Montana fought numerous injuries that sidelined him for a significant amount of time. Each time, he came back, usually playing with pain.

In the 1989 playoffs, Montana was at his absolute best as the 49ers whipped two quality teams—the Minnesota Vikings and Chicago Bears—before wrecking the Broncos in the Super Bowl.

"We took command of the game so early that it was a surprise to people," Montana said of Super Bowl XXIV. "We were ahead by three touchdowns [27–3] and everything was going perfectly." By the time the 49ers had taken a 20–3 lead, they had run 37 plays to merely 17 for the Broncos. The 49ers were clicking on offense and defense. With 1:38 left in the first half, Montana went to the long ball for the first time in the game, a 38-yard TD pass to Rice. That gave the 49ers a 27–3 lead that buried the Broncos.

The touchdowns were coming so frequently that Montana continued to use the same long-ball tactics in the second half. Another long pass gave the 49ers a 41–3 lead and wrapped up the rout. Montana completed a record five touchdown passes, three to Rice, in the 55–10 win. Montana won his fourth Super Bowl in four tries, while Broncos quarterback John Elway lost his third in three tries.

"I had all day to throw," Montana said. "I only got touched twice—once when I scrambled out of bounds."

Montana completed 22 of 29 passes for 297 yards as he set a record with 13 straight pass completions, one of his five records in the game.

"He's got this resourcefulness, this something that's hard to put into words, that enables him to perform well under pressure," Walsh told *Sports Illustrated*. "And he will not choke."

Montana finished his NFL career in 1994 with the Kansas City Chiefs following a 16-year run that featured 40,551 yards and a 63.2 percent pass completion rate.

In 2006, he was chosen by *Sports Illustrated* as the number 1 clutch quarterback of all time.

THE 1990s

Super Bowl XXV

THERE WERE SEVERAL BIG STARS AT THE 25TH SUPER BOWL IN TAMPA.

In the midst of the Gulf War, Whitney Houston belted out the most memorable rendition of "The Star-Spangled Banner" that anyone on hand could remember. The fact she lip-synched a previously recorded version didn't lessen the impact—nor was it noticed by the 73,813 fans on hand or the millions watching on TV.

"Didn't matter," Bills center Kent Hull once said. "It was great."

And there were Giants coaches Bill Parcells and Bill Belichick, who masterminded a defense that turned the K-Gun Offense into something of a pop gun. Using a variety of alignments, including several with only two defensive linemen, the Giants befuddled the league's highest-scoring attack, one that ripped through Oakland for 51 points in the AFC championship game. That Super Bowl game plan made its way to the Pro Football Hall of Fame.

Of course, there was the collection of defensive stars who made such strategy work: all-world linebacker Lawrence Taylor, linemen Leonard Marshall and Erik Howard, and backs Everson Walls and Greg Jackson.

There was Jeff Hostetler, a backup quarterback to Phil Simms for Hostetler's first four pro seasons and for most of 1990. Then Simms broke his leg—against Buffalo, no less—in Game 14, and any charge to the championship would need to be guided by "Hoss." He did so admirably, raising his record as a Giant to 4-0 in regular-season games, then helping them beat Chicago and San Francisco in the playoffs.

Most of all, when Whitney was done singing, and the crowd was done raising its voice in patriotic fervor, there was Ottis Anderson, all 6'2", 220 pounds of him, battering the Bills. "I remember [offensive coordinator] Ron Erhardt come over and sit down next to me," Anderson recalled. "He said, 'We're going to run you and run you, I need you to give me all you got. We're going to wear them down. Let's just go ram the ball.' That's what our plan was."

Not at all a bad plan. "A good offense is a good defense," Anderson said, "and a good defense is keeping the ball away from Jim Kelly."

The veteran Anderson, a Parcells favorite who was the 1979 Offensive Rookie of the Year with the Cardinals, had spent much of his career rushing for more than 1,100 yards and as much as 1,605 on mediocre or worse St. Louis squads. He joined the Giants midway through the 1986 campaign and was mostly a backup until 1989, when he rushed for 1,023 yards and 14 touchdowns and was elected the NFL's Comeback Player of the Year. So Anderson was ready for his star turn in the big game.

He bulled his way to 102 yards and one touchdown. His collisions, most notably with Bills safety Mark Kelso, were a case of classic power football—just what the Giants wanted.

"I was trying to figure out how can I make you think about hitting me," Anderson said. "All day long, Kelso and I kept running into each other and we'd collide, and he would go, 'Uh, Uh,' and I would say, 'OK, OK.'

"If I could intimidate him into thinking I was really going to tear his head off, then he wouldn't think about how to tackle me."

Even with Anderson's performance, the Giants needed "Wide Right," a missed 47-yard field goal by Scott Norwood as the clock ran out, to survive. In many ways, Norwood's miss has become the most infamous in Super Bowl lore and has overshadowed Anderson. Fans in Buffalo will tell you if Norwood had been accurate, the Bills would have won four straight Super Bowls, not lost all of them.

Anderson can only smile when the subject is brought up. And then flash his championship ring.

Super Bowl XXVI

Most teams who frequent the Super Bowl over a short span are guided by the same quarterback. You know, Starr and Tarkenton and Staubach. Bradshaw and Montana. Aikman and Brady.

Not the Washington Redskins. In a span of nine years, they went to four Super Bowls behind three different quarterbacks. Credit the coaching acumen of Joe Gibbs for knowing how to put together a contender regardless of who was behind center. Also credit Gibbs for getting the most out of decent but not outstanding QBs who happened to fit the Gibbs offense well.

He won a lot of games with Joe Theismann, Jay Schroeder, Doug Williams, and, in 1991, Mark Rypien. A sixth-round draftee out of Washington State and that rare Canadian passer who makes it to the NFL, Rypien took a circuitous route to the starting job. "I played hockey before I played football," he said, although his family moved to Spokane when he was five.

Rypien was one of many raw players with plenty of upside that teams would stash on injured reserve in the 1980s, when the roster rules were much less strict than they became in later years. So Rypien spent his first two pro seasons on IR, first with a knee injury, then a back problem. No one was sure when (or if) he got hurt, and Gibbs wasn't saying. In the meantime, as Rypien said, "I was learning the offense, learning what my teammates could do, understanding Coach Gibbs' game plans."

And in 1989, Gibbs turned to Rypien, who went 16-8 in his starts during his first two seasons, despite plenty of complaints that he was sporadic, his arm was a scatter gun, and he didn't like to be hit in the pocket (what quarterback does?).

In 1991, Rypien evolved into a second-team All-Pro behind Buffalo's Jim Kelly. Washington went 14-2 as Rypien threw for 28 TDs with 11 interceptions, and the Redskins scored 485 points. Not even the Bills with their vaunted K-Gun Offense could match that, and the Redskins had a strong defense to boot, yielding only 224 points, less than everyone but New Orleans.

Rypien had to have dangerous targets and productive runners operating behind solid blockers to score what was then a record number of points. Washington had all that, from the Hogs on the offensive line, to the three-headed RB corps of Earnest Byner (1,048 yards rushing), Ricky Ervins, and Gerald Riggs (11 TDs), to the Fun Bunch—wideouts Art Monk, a future Hall of Famer, Ricky Sanders, and Gary Clark.

The defense was led by another player headed to the Canton shrine, cornerback Darrell Green, and sackmaster Charles Mann. "We had everything you could want on that team," Green said. "We felt unbeatable when we took the field."

Atlanta and Detroit couldn't touch them in the NFC playoffs, but the Bills supposedly were another story. They'd barely lost the previous Super Bowl on Scott Norwood's missed 47-yard field goal at the gun. They clearly were the best team in the AFC, a maturing group under a Hall of Fame coach, Marv Levy. And they pretty much never had a shot.

"We can beat you a lot of ways," said Gary Clark, who had seven receptions for 114 yards and one score. "We'll use whatever it takes, and we've got what it takes. We jumped on them right away, and there was no looking back."

No reason to in the NFC's eighth straight Super Bowl victory. From the very outset, when Bills running back and league MVP Thurman Thomas couldn't find his helmet on the sideline and didn't start, until the 37–24 romp was completed, it pretty much was all Washington. And mostly due to Rypien.

Sure, he had loads of help. Riggs did his thing with two short touchdown runs as the Redskins built a 17–0 halftime edge and a 24–0 lead in the third quarter. The line kept Bruce Smith, the eventual career sacks leader, from doing any damage. The defense held Buffalo's top-ranked offense to eight yards rushing in the first half, sacked Kelly five times in the contest, and picked off four passes.

Rypien's mastery behind center earned him the MVP trophy, something he wanted to divide up. "For all of us, we can strut around for the next four or five months with the idea that we're the best in the game. We can take it everywhere. For me, there were 45 MVPs."

But there was one who could especially savor this championship after much criticism of his playing style and performances in the past few years.

Rypien simply shrugged when asked about redemption. "I don't hold grudges," Rypien said. "They were right and maybe the criticism helped me make the right decisions. Maybe they made me address them and make myself a better player.

"But you know what? They can't say that anymore. They can't say he didn't win the big one. If there's one bigger than this one, I haven't heard about it."

Super Bowl XXVII-XXVIII

Emmitt Smith sat back in his chair and flashed that contagious smile that has always come easily to the most prolific running back in NFL history. Then he just as easily came up with the answers to two key questions about his Hall of Fame career.

Q: What were the highlights of your years with the Cowboys?

A: "Winning Super Bowls, of course."

Q: Any of those three particularly special?

A: "All of them. There's nothing like it than walking off that field knowing you are at the top, the very best, and no one can doubt it."

Three times in a four-year span, Smith and the Cowboys did exactly that. In those Super Bowl victories over Buffalo in 1993 and 1994 and against Pittsburgh in 1996, Smith combined for 289 yards rushing, 56 receiving, and, most notably, five TDs. He had the winning score in the second and third championship victories.

As the fulcrum of the Triplets—the Cowboys' three-pronged attack that also included future Hall of Famers Troy Aikman at quarterback and Michael Irvin at wideout—Smith was the go-to guy in so many ways. On and off the field.

Need some insightful quotes and thoughts? Try Emmitt.

Leadership? Go to number 22.

Resourcefulness? Smith left Florida early, but in 1996, he earned his college degree, fulfilling a promise he made to his mother.

Dependability? On his way to becoming the career rushing leader and only player to gain more than 18,000 yards on the ground, Smith was the first with five straight 1,400-yard rushing seasons and the first with 11 consecutive 1,000-yard campaigns. That dependable enough?

If not, try this: At the end of the 1993 season, with the defending league champion Cowboys in a dogfight with the Giants for the NFC East title, they met at the Meadowlands. The winner would finish 12-4, taking the division crown, becoming the favorite to represent the conference in the Super Bowl.

Smith, who held out for a new contract and missed the opening two games of the schedule—Dallas dropped both of them and owner Jerry Jones rapidly capitulated to his star running back's demands—would be the key to a Dallas win in the wind and cold of northern New Jersey.

Late in the opening half, Smith broke free for a 46-yard gain. Heavy-hitting safety Greg Jackson brought him down to the rock-hard turf, Smith falling on his right shoulder. And staying down.

"Something happened in my shoulder that I never felt before," he said later. "I had never known pain like that."

When you separate your shoulder, well, it does kind of hurt, Emmitt.

"They told me I could sit out the rest of the game or I could actually play because I couldn't do any more damage," he recalled. "But I had to be able to deal with the pain. I wasn't sitting out anything when they said that."

The trainers invented a bulked-up shoulder pad by putting knee pads in it and cutting a hole in the middle. After taking a pain-killing shot during halftime, Smith was back on the field—talking to himself.

"I kept telling myself the same thing: 'There's no pain, there's no pain,'" he said with an ironic laugh, because there was plenty of pain.

Had the Cowboys kept dominating the action, Smith would have had an easier time in the second half. Instead, New York surged back. A touchdown and two field goals tied it 13–13 and the teams headed to overtime. Just what Smith needed, more football.

Playing basically with one arm in the second half, Smith overall carried 32 times and made 10 receptions. The Giants clearly targeted his injured shoulder, as any opponent would, yet he kept coming. Even when coach Jimmy Johnson suggested Smith play a decoy role, the running back screamed back, "If I can play, let me play."

On the Cowboys' 52-yard drive to a winning field goal, Smith was in on nine plays, gained 41 yards, and even stiff-armed all-world linebacker Lawrence Taylor on one run.

After the game, Aikman called it "the most courageous performance I have ever been a part of in football."

So when Smith went on to lead the Cowboys past Green Bay and San Francisco and into the Super Bowl in Atlanta, who could be surprised? Smith still was hampered by the shoulder in those two playoff victories. Come Super Bowl XXVIII, and knowing he would undergo surgery after one more heroic effort, Smith was unstoppable against Buffalo.

Remaining the workhorse, he carried 30 times for 130 yards and two touchdowns—the decisive TD and the clinching one—to earn MVP honors in a 30–13 victory over the Bills.

"I had the best seat in the house," Aikman said. "I rarely ever saw the first guy who made contact with him bring him to the ground. Sometimes, we would have free tacklers right in the hole, but rarely did that guy make the tackle. He had an amazing ability to make people miss."

Just a year earlier, it was Aikman who couldn't miss in a 52–17 laugher over Buffalo for the Cowboys' first championship since beating Denver in the 1978 game. Yes, the Bills resembled the Keystone Cops throughout their much-less-than-Super performance at the Rose Bowl. They committed nine turnovers; it could have been worse but Buffalo recovered three of its fumbles.

Aikman was a surgeon, completing 22 of 30 passes for 273 yards and four touchdowns. Had he needed to do so, Aikman could have thrown for another four or so.

For Aikman, bringing home the Lombardi Trophy and the MVP award from the Super Bowl was the culmination of a relatively short climb that to him must have felt years longer.

The NFL's top overall draft choice in 1989—the first player selected by Johnson and new Cowboys owner Jones—out of UCLA (by way of Oklahoma, where he spent his first two college years), Aikman went from overmatched to overwhelming.

In '89, when he was healthy and not riding the bench behind Steve Walsh, Aikman was a not-so-impressive 0-11. Dallas went 1-15, and the football world laughed at the collegiate approach Johnson was bringing to the pros.

"That was a tough time," Aikman said. "Players would be there one week and gone the next."

The 1990 season was better, but Aikman went only 7-8 and threw seven more picks than TDs. In '91, the Cowboys returned to the post-season at 11-5, but Aikman's numbers were pedestrian and Dallas was blown out in the second round of the playoffs by Detroit.

"Troy came to the Cowboys at a time when they [the fans] needed a hero," Johnson told *D* magazine. "The Cowboys were last in the league. He was the All-American college quarterback, good-looking, single. And I think a lot of people in Dallas identified with Troy as the person who was going to help them bring back championships."

But when? The coming of age for Aikman and the rest of the Cowboys under the JJs (Jimmy Johnson and Jerry Jones) came the next year.

"We had no one pointing us in the right direction," guard Kevin Gogan said. "He was the right person to take over."

Dallas went 13-3 during the 1992 season. Aikman led the NFL in completion percentage, threw only six interceptions, and in the NFC title game at San Francisco, he outplayed league MVP Steve Young.

He trumped that in the Super Bowl, throwing three first-half TD passes, four in all. Early on, though, it was a struggle. Not against Buffalo's sieve of a defense, but against nerves.

"Going out and seeing the pageantry of it, I had to talk myself into relaxing," Aikman said. "Early on, I was caught up in the moment and too anxious. I didn't feel real comfortable until midway through the second quarter. Then I got into a groove.

"It's as great a feeling as I've ever had in my life," Aikman added of earning a championship. "I wish every player could experience it."

He, Smith, and the rest of the Cowboys would experience it two more times in the next three seasons as they established a Big D dynasty.

Super Bowl XXIX

STEVE YOUNG HAD HEARD IT ALL.

He wasn't Joe Montana.

He didn't win the big ones, which Super Joe never lost.

He was a left-handed scrambler, and those quarterbacks don't win championships.

Young, among the most intelligent, insightful, and outgoing football players anyone could meet, recognized how to answer the critics. Do what his predecessor with the 49ers had accomplished—and a little more.

His answer came in the 1994 season, and then in a mismatch of a Super Bowl in Miami.

The NFL's Most Valuable Player that season, Young cemented his Hall of Fame resume with a big-game performance for the ages: 25 for 38 for 331 yards, no interceptions, and six touchdown passes. Oh, he also rushed for 49 yards, and San Francisco scored 49 points.

Masterful would be an understatement. Redemptive would not.

"There were many days a few years ago when I'd get to work and want to just turn around because it was so difficult," Young told the *Philadelphia Daily News*. "For one person to face the kind of scrutiny and skepticism and tough times [that I did] . . . it's so rewarding that I was able to play through that and stand here today. It's just a spectacular feeling."

Following a legend is difficult enough. Young had the misfortune of being cast in the role of usurper, which was hardly accurate: He played in 1991 and '92 for San Francisco mostly because Montana was not healthy.

All Young did was lead the NFL in passer rating in those two seasons. He did so again in '93 with Montana having moved on to Kansas City. And yet again in '94, his second MVP year.

But there were no Super Bowl trips in those years. Hardly Montanan, if you will.

"All along, I thought I was playing great football. I had the critics and skeptics backpedaling. I had them backpedaling pretty fast.

"But they still had this game to fall back on. If we didn't beat the Chargers, they'd say I couldn't win the Big One.

"It's nice to finally put it away, put it to rest."

Young put it to rest early. San Francisco was a 19-point favorite, the biggest spread in the game's history. It took all of three plays to make this one history.

Young and all-universe receiver Jerry Rice noticed on that third play that San Diego's alignment meant a linebacker would be covering Rice if he ran a route to the middle of the field. Ten linebackers at once couldn't cover Rice.

The result: a 44-yard touchdown pass, a 7–0 lead—and the rout was on.

Young never let up, as if each completion, each TD, was further proof of his value. In a way, it was: the culmination of an ascent that deserved far more applause than admonishment.

By halftime, it was 28–10. Soon after, 42–10. Rice would finish with 10 catches and 149 yards—of course—in receptions. Three of his receptions went for touchdowns.

Young didn't do it alone, naturally. Rickey Watters rushed for a touchdown and caught two of Young's TD passes. Deion Sanders, rented for the season, had a pick on a defense that rarely let the Chargers breathe, let alone compete.

For Young, the 49–26 victory was a crowning moment in a career that, like Montana, would lead him to the Hall of Fame.

"There will be people who will never be satisfied," center Bart Oates said. "There will be diehards who will say Steve's only won one [Super Bowl] and Joe won four. Joe Montana had a great run and did great things for the 49ers franchise."

The torch was passed to Steve Young, who went out and created an era of his own.

Super Bowl XXX

Larry Brown is one of the most serviceable names in pro sports. At some point in time, there has been a Larry Brown on a professional roster in all four major team sports.

The Larry Brown of Super Bowl lore was a solid cornerback for the Cowboys. Not a superstar—the other starting cornerback in Super Bowl XXX owned that role, Deion Sanders—but dependable.

And on this Sunday in the Valley of the Sun for the first Super Bowl staged in Arizona, Brown was, well, everything Dallas had signed free agent Sanders to be.

For Brown, 1995 was a difficult year marked by tragedy. His two-month-old son, Kristopher, died from complications after a premature birth.

"If you look at the personal aspect of it, Larry and his wife are kids themselves," Cowboys owner Jerry Jones said. "It just breaks your heart to see young people have to share a burden that a lot of people 30 and 40 years older than them have never shared.

"They had to deal through that. There was a tremendous outpouring on our team for Larry."

Brown also found strength in the memory of Kristopher. He grabbed six interceptions, one fewer than his career total in four previous NFL seasons, and scored two touchdowns.

"I had to get back in uniform and suit up," he said. "I felt I needed to play. I didn't have to play. The organization did not put any pressure on me. My family and I decided that it would be best if I played and it worked out for me.

"It was rough, but with the team and the players and the way they supported me through all of the hard times," Brown added, "I've just got to give them credit. I couldn't have done it without them. They enabled me to get through this season."

Opposing quarterbacks went after Brown because, frankly, they feared Sanders's cover skills. Just as frankly, Brown was the better cover man against first-rate receivers for portions of that season.

In the Super Bowl, he was the difference maker. Dallas built 13–0 and 20–7 leads thanks in great part to the renowned Triplets: Troy Aikman threw for a touchdown, Emmitt Smith ran for one, and Michael Irvin kept the latest rendition of the Steel Curtain off-balance with his receptions. Yet the two biggest plays on a star-studded roster that included six future Hall of Famers came from Larry Brown.

With Dallas leading 13–7, Neil O'Donnell went into the shotgun and threw to, uh, no one can be certain because the ball went straight at Brown at the Dallas 38 yard line.

Brown scooted 44 yards to the Pittsburgh 18. Two plays later, it was 20–7.

But the Steelers scored 10 straight points and got the ball back with 4:15 remaining in regulation. From his 32, O'Donnell, in the shotgun again, found Brown again. Brown returned the pick 22 yards to the Steelers 6.

"I had to go get it," he said. "I made a great break on the ball. The slant was coming and I beat the receiver to it. They try to throw everything on timing and I was just able to get there first."

Smith scored from the 4 and Dallas had its fifth Lombardi Trophy, tying San Francisco for the most at the time.

And Brown had MVP honors.

"I saw my name on the scoreboard," he said. "Everybody on the team started chanting 'Larry! Larry!' I was excited and happy. It's something I'll cherish for the rest of my life."

A life that was about to get very busy and very lucrative. "I'm doing interviews with [David] Letterman, [Conan] O'Brien and [Jay] Leno," he said. "Kathie Lee [Gifford] and Regis [Philbin] is Thursday. It's a full schedule. I'll be 'Hollywood' now."

Close. He signed a five-year, $12.5 million contract with the Raiders, who apparently believed they were getting the next Deion. Even before he'd finished one of his three disappointing seasons in Oakland, though, Brown had filed for bankruptcy.

He had one interception in 16 games for the Raiders, wound up getting suspended by Oakland for conduct detrimental to the team, and eventually was arrested on 18 counts of writing bad checks at Las Vegas casinos. He was released after agreeing to pay nearly $44,000 in debts.

A sad ending to a previously uplifting personal saga.

Super Bowl XXXI

HEISMAN TROPHY RECIPIENTS HAVE HAD A MIXED HISTORY IN THE pros.

Heisman winners who mimic the statue's pose before actually winning it, well, the first one of those was a decent NFL player—and a Super Bowl hero.

Desmond Howard was one of the greatest players for the storied football program at Michigan. In 1991, he was so dynamic as a receiver and kick returner that he outshined all the quarterbacks and running backs throughout the nation. It was a rare triumph for a wideout, and Howard remains the last at the position to take the Heisman.

From Michigan, he headed to the NFL as the fourth overall pick, by Washington.

Howard barely made a mark in the nation's capital, with only 66 receptions and five touchdowns over three seasons. Used in a variety of ways, his biggest contributions came returning kicks, but by 1995, he was a Jaguar.

His stint in Jacksonville lasted all of one pedestrian season. Questions about his ability to adapt his game to the pros, a lack of burst off the line of scrimmage as a receiver, and his size (5'10", 185) plagued Howard.

Then he landed in Green Bay; talk about storied franchises.

Howard's timing was perfect. The Packers, with rising star Brett Favre at quarterback and the Minister of Defense, Reggie White, leading his unit, were ready for a return to Super Bowl glory. Their last trip to the big game had been in 1968 when, under Vince Lombardi, the Packers won their second straight Super Bowl. After that, zilch.

And Howard's timing was awful, too. Already strong at receiver, Green Bay picked him up to spark the special teams. But Howard got hurt in the preseason, and Packers coach Mike Holmgren wasn't sure he could find a place on the roster for Howard.

"We wanted him to be our guy returning kicks," Holmgren said. "We felt he could really contribute there, but he couldn't stay on the field in the [preseason] games."

Howard's job was saved by the fact the Packers were so strong elsewhere. They felt they could carry him, but he needed to get healthy. And then Howard needed to find some of that Heisman magic.

"There were a lot of lessons to be learned. Great teammates man," Howard told the *New Orleans Times-Picayune*. "People don't understand how valuable that is to a person like myself. I'm all about the team and I'm never about any individualism. Brett Favre, the late, great Reggie White. Those were some Hall of Famers and I just wanted to do my part."

His part was to produce on the most exciting of football plays: kick returns. Howard came through. In the 1996 season, as the Packers went 13-3, Howard ran back 58 punts for an outstanding, league-best 15.1-yard average and scored three touchdowns. He handled 22 kickoff returns, too, averaging 20.9 yards a return.

"Field position," he said. "My job was to help us with field position, and if I broke a few, then great."

When the Packers arrived in New Orleans for Super Bowl XXXI as a 14-point favorite, many of the headlines centered on their opponent. New England coach Bill Parcells was hotly rumored to be ready to leave because he did not have enough say in the Patriots' personnel moves. Parcells even uttered this famous line about the pending divorce: "They want you to cook the dinner, at least they should let you shop for the groceries."

Howard had a 71-yard TD punt return in a playoff win over San Francisco. In a massive understatement, Parcells said of Howard: "We need to watch him, he's dangerous." Dangerous enough that Howard could become a game changer in this Super Bowl. Even the folks from Disney World who honored the MVP with a trip to their Magic Kingdom recognized that.

Brett Favre

When the Packers traded a first-round draft pick to Atlanta for some backup quarterback named Brett Favre, you could have melted the midwinter tundra at Lambeau Field with the heat Green Bay general manager Ron Wolf took.

But Wolf recognized a raw talent who, with the right guidance and a huge touch of maturity, could be a franchise quarterback.

A second-round selection in 1991, Favre had flopped in his only season in the ATL. Jerry Glanville, then the Falcons' coach, noted that Favre was a party guy, not a football guy, as a rookie.

What Wolf saw, particularly during a pregame throwing session before the Packers played the Falcons that year, was "the guy."

"It was done with a lot of thought," Wolf said of the trade. "To me the most important thing in professional football is having a person at that position. I think we've got a future here in this guy."

Some future. While Favre would reach only two Super Bowls and win one—he threw for two long TDs and ran for a short one in the 35–21 victory against New England—he became a slam-dunk Hall of Fame quarterback in his illustrious 20-season career with the Packers, Jets, and Vikings. When he at last quit in 2011 after several premature retirements, Favre held virtually every significant passing record in the books.

Had it not been for the Howard Heroics at the Superdome, Favre might well have walked off with MVP honors. Aside from Howard's scintillating kickoff return TD, the lasting image of Super Bowl XXXI is of Favre ripping off his helmet and racing downfield after his early TD throw to Andre Rison.

"Every game he came running out of that tunnel, ready to give everything he had for this franchise and its fans," longtime Packers CEO Bob Harlan said. "He was the greatest competitor I've ever been around, and he played with the passion and enthusiasm of a kid on the sandlot."

Howard told the *Times-Picayune* that they knocked on his hotel door the morning of the game to "explain protocol" for whomever was voted Most Valuable Player. "I was flattered by it, but that was the furthest thing from my mind," Howard said. "I was just trying to win the game and get a ring. We are out there playing for that jewelry.

"I was flattered by it, so it crossed somebody's mind. I'll be damned if it didn't happen."

You bet.

The Packers led 27–21 after Patriots running back Curtis Martin scored on an 18-yard run in the third quarter. On the next kickoff, Heisman Howard reappeared. He caught the ball at the 1, sprinted up the middle of the field, brushed off a tackle at the 28, and, as Pat Summerall described it on TV: "He's gone." So were New England's chances.

Howard finished with 244 yards in returns, and the Packers won 35–21. And a special teams player was the MVP.

"It makes for a tremendous story, a guy who was on the cusp of being released and his final act was he walked away with the Super Bowl MVP," said Howard, who played another six seasons without approaching the success of the 1996 season. "I don't know if it gets any better than that. I really don't think so."

Super Bowl XXXII-XXXIII

JOHN ELWAY HAD NO CHANCE IN THE SUPER BOWL UNTIL TERRELL Davis came along.

And where, exactly, did Davis come from?

Few teammates could have had more varying football backgrounds than Denver's quarterback and running back in what turned into the glory days for the Broncos.

Elway was the rocket-armed top overall draft pick in 1983, the first of six quarterbacks chosen in the opening round. An All-America QB from Stanford, also a baseball prospect, Elway drew headlines before he ever took a snap as a pro, refusing to consider signing with the Colts (then in Baltimore). He forced a trade to Denver, then led the Broncos out of the Rockies and into three Super Bowls in four years (the 1986, '87, and '89 seasons). All ended in Super failures.

While Elway was the BMOC pretty much his entire life, Davis was pretty much an afterthought. He played one season at Long Beach State and three more at Georgia, showing a penchant for finding the end zone with 21 touchdowns in his college career. But his 1,919 yards rushing over those four seasons hardly screamed out superstar to NFL scouts.

It took 196 picks for Davis to hear his name in the 1995 draft. It didn't take long for him to grab the running back job and run over people with it.

"Some people said TD came from nowhere," said Broncos tight end Shannon Sharpe. "Doesn't matter where he came from, it matters where he's going."

Where he was going was to the mountaintop of the NFL.

Davis was the 1996 Offensive Player of the Year, an award he would win again in 1998 when he became the fourth player to rush for at least 2,000 yards (2,008). Even more significantly, his Broncos also were headed for the summit.

Of course, they'd been close before, thanks greatly to Elway. But the final step was too slippery until Davis brought the balance Denver needed.

"The thing about the Broncos," Green Bay coach Mike Holmgren said before the teams met in Super Bowl XXXII in San Diego, "is they can beat you in so many ways. When they've got the ball, it's sort of which poison, the passing game with John, or the running game with Terrell Davis." In the 1998 Super Bowl, it was clear who was more infectious. Davis rushed 30 times for 157 yards and three touchdowns against the 12-point favorite and defending champion Packers. Elway was efficient, avoiding the critical mistakes that doomed the Broncos in his previous three Super Bowls.

But Davis gave Green Bay headaches all day, so appropriate because he played much of the game with a migraine. Migraines had plagued Davis since childhood, one reason he never was a dominant collegian. In the Super Sunday buildup and excitement, Davis simply forgot to take his medication. Davis was fine until the first big hit of the game, his helmet colliding with a defender's knee. "I remember it was just like a blunt force, like 'BAM!'" he said. "And it just kind of rocked my world."

Coach Mike Shanahan, fully aware of how Green Bay would key on his star runner, asked Davis if he could act as a decoy. "I could see enough to get out of someone's way," Davis said. "It was about doing what I could do to help us win the game. I didn't think twice about it. I wasn't thinking about self-preservation."

Yet Davis was on his way to Super Bowl MVP honors. Through Davis, Denver controlled the tempo. Its defense kept Brett Favre and the Packers off-balance just enough. TD scored on three 1-yard runs, the final touchdown in the 31–24 victory tinted with controversy.

After Davis's 17-yard jaunt to the Green Bay 1, with just under two minutes remaining, Holmgren ordered the unorthodox from his defense: Let Denver score.

"It was a strategy I felt was our only chance to win," Holmgren said, reasoning the Broncos would run down the clock and kick a field goal with a few seconds left had the Packers not stepped aside and let Davis surge into the end zone.

While it was totally unexpected to hear such a command from the sideline, Packers safety Eugene Robinson understood. "I thought that was pretty smart because I said, 'We need valuable time,'" Robinson said. "And I talked to John Elway. He said, 'Yeah, we scored!' And I said, 'Yeah, we're trying to get the ball back.'"

Which the Pack did. And Favre guided them to the Denver 31 before John Mobley tipped Favre's fourth-down pass with 28 seconds remaining.

That Super stigma as losers was gone for the Broncos and for Elway, who'd survived a tackle by one of the sport's best hitters, Packers safety LeRoy Butler, that sent Elway spinning in the air like a runaway helicopter.

"I know that I've been labeled as the guy who's never been on the winning Super Bowl team," an exultant Elway said. "Boy, am I glad to get rid of that."

Now that Elway had done so, was he himself done with the NFL? He waited several months before telling Shanahan and the organization his plans. He was coming back.

"The bottom line is I wasn't ready to quit competing," Elway said. "I've got a lot of years to live in retirement and the last thing I want to do is pass up the opportunity to play one more year of football."

The Elway Farewell Tour was quite a show. Through September, October, and November, beyond Thanksgiving, the Broncos didn't lose. Led by Davis's brilliant runs on his way to league MVP honors, and Elway's passing and leadership, the offense was unstoppable, averaging more than 33 points a game. They were 13-0 when they visited the Meadowlands to face a mediocre Giants team, and talk of an undefeated campaign was rampant.

The Broncos tried to ignore or play down all of the chatter, and after the Giants stunned them, 21–20, Shanahan almost seemed relieved that the pressure of seeking perfection was gone. But he was downright annoyed the following week when the Broncos fell again, to Miami.

He need not have worried. Denver won its season finale to finish 14-2, then beat the Dolphins and the Jets to reach a second straight Super Bowl.

A matchup with the powerhouse Vikings had been expected in the title game, but Minnesota stumbled at home in overtime in the NFC championship game. Instead, Atlanta qualified, its first trip to the Super Bowl.

The Falcons flopped 34–19 as Elway threw for 336 yards and a touchdown, ran for another, and walked off with MVP honors.

Then he walked away.

"I don't look at it as retirement," Elway said. "I'm just graduating from pro football."

Elway's career conclusion was much more enjoyable than what Davis went through. In his fourth game of 1999, Davis's knee was wrecked, and the injury never fully healed. By the end of the 2001 season, he was done as a player.

Davis wound up being the first of a slew of running backs Shanahan plugged in and got impressive production from. The list of 1,000-yard guys includes Mike Anderson, Olandis Gary, Clinton Portis, and Reuben Droughns. Only Portis came with high expectations.

None of them could match Davis's magnificent four-year span of achievement. Nor his Super Bowl rings.

"There have been a lot of 1,500-yard rushers in this league and guys who won MVP awards, but there haven't been very many guys that run for 2,000 yards and win the MVP and the Super Bowl," Sharpe said when asked if Davis belongs in the Hall of Fame, a place Sharpe entered in 2011. "I don't think you can say because he didn't play for 10 or 15 years that he shouldn't get in. From 1996–98, he was the best player in the game, bar none."

THE NEW MILLENNIUM

Super Bowl XXXIV

WHEN YOU'RE STOCKING GROCERY SHELVES WITH WHAT YOU BELIEVE IS a million-dollar arm, the Super Bowl is a fantasy.

Welcome to Kurt Warner's world.

Nothing in Warner's trek to the NFL indicated he would ever be a difference maker, particularly on football's biggest stage. Yes, he had that cannon of a right arm, but he so failed to impress NFL scouts—or even Division I college programs—that Warner was a rank outsider.

He went to Northern Iowa, a Division I-AA school at the time, with a solid resume on that level, but hardly an NFL prospects factory. Warner sat on the bench his first three years at Northern Iowa, almost quitting college. As a senior, he became the starter and wound up conference player of the year.

Still, he wasn't drafted, got an invite to training camp with the Packers that lasted only five weeks, then became something of a gridiron nomad. Arena Football. NFL Europe. A backup job behind sturdy Trent Green with the Rams.

Then came a serious knee injury in preseason to Green. What to do? Coach Dick Vermeil stuck with the untested Warner. "Kurt Warner has a lot of attributes and has paid his dues," said Vermeil. "He has never been given a good enough opportunity. We will rally around Kurt Warner."

Magic ensued. Hard-earned magic.

"Sure, I had my tough times, but you don't sit there and say, 'Wow, I was stocking groceries five years ago, and look at me now,'" Warner said. "You don't think about it, and when you do achieve something, you know luck has nothing to do with it."

An NFL also-ran since moving from Los Angeles to St. Louis after the 1994 season, the Rams were the longest of long shots in 1999 to do anything special. And then everything clicked.

Warner's experience behind center in the Arena League, where he set passing records, and in Europe had led to a maturation of his game. He could read defenses. He could inspire teammates.

And he had that bazooka to get the ball to Isaac Bruce, Torry Holt, and Marshall Faulk.

St. Louis won its first six games, lost two, then won seven in a row. A 13-3 record earned the Rams top seed in the NFC, and they beat Minnesota and Tampa Bay in the playoffs.

Shockingly, Warner was a Super Bowl QB. And, to boot, the NFL's Most Valuable Player.

"I thought we could be successful," Warner said, "but to think in training camp that it would happen for me this way was pretty farfetched. They were not sure what they would do going in, they had some questions if I was an NFL backup."

Backup? He was 1999's best player, and he put the finishing touches on a true rags-to-hero story with his performance in Atlanta against the Titans.

The city was in the midst of such severe weather—ice storms, snow, wind—that no Super Bowl has gone back to Atlanta since. Early in the week, Tennessee's players met the media in a large tent that was not heated; they wore overcoats for the interviews.

Meanwhile, the Rams were holding their news conferences in an indoor ballroom. Must have been an omen.

Warner didn't need to do much in the first half, leading the Rams on three scoring drives capped by Jeff Wilkins kicking field goals of 27, 28, and 28 yards. Warner opened second-half scoring with a 9-yard pass to Holt for a 16–0 edge.

If anyone understood things rarely go so easily, though, it was Warner. And back stormed the Titans.

"They were AFC champs, they were a great opponent that wasn't going to lay down," he said. "They showed their true spirit when they came back."

Mike Jones

In his 13 pro seasons, many of them as a backup, Mike Jones was a significant if not crucial part of defenses for the Raiders, Rams, and Steelers.

On January 31, 2000, he was a Super Bowl hero.

A versatile player with a nose for the ball, Jones had one of his best NFL seasons. He even scored three touchdowns.

Preventing touchdowns was his, and any defender's, calling, of course. As the Titans rallied from a 16–0 deficit against an increasingly tiring St. Louis D in Super Bowl XXXIV, Jones seemed an unlikely savior.

Tennessee tied it with just over two minutes remaining, but only 18 seconds later, Kurt Warner connected with Isaac Bruce on a 73-yard heave for a 23–16 lead. "They gave us the lead and we had to go out and protect it," Jones said.

Except the Titans inexorably moved the ball downfield, reaching the Rams 6 in the dying seconds. One play to tie it and force the first Super Bowl OT. Or maybe even have Tennessee go for a two-point conversion to win it.

Up stepped Jones.

On the final play of regulation, Steve McNair was forced to throw underneath to Kevin Dyson short of the goal line. The idea was simple: the slippery Dyson would elude the linebacker covering him—Jones.

But Jones had sniffed out the play. "I think they thought we thought they were going to the end zone," Jones said. "They thought they would catch us two yards back in the end zone and they'd dive and get in.

"When he caught the ball I knew he was short of the end zone a couple yards. I was right on top of him and I knew that all I had to do was get him down. That's what I did."

Just as coach Dick Vermeil would have predicted. "He is just one of those kind of guys, and he has made a ton of plays all year," Vermeil said. Including one of the biggest in franchise history.

"You dream of making an interception or a sack, not necessarily a tackle to win the game," Jones said. "But we'll take that."

Eddie George ran for two short touchdowns—one extra point failed—and Al Del Greco tied it with a 43-yard field goal with just 2:12 on the clock.

Was the first Super Bowl overtime at hand?

It didn't take long for Warner to answer: 18 seconds. He dropped back and unleashed a long pass for Bruce that was a bit short. Cornerback Denard Walker fell, and Bruce caught the ball and bolted into the end zone for a 73-yard score.

"Isaac is our go-to guy," said Warner, who wound up with a then–Super Bowl record 414 yards passing. "He's made big plays for us all year and we knew he could make another one."

The Rams would need another one (see sidebar) to preserve their unlikely title.

Meanwhile, Warner's wondrous season wound up being anything but a fluke. He would win another league MVP award for 2001, again guiding the Rams to the Super Bowl. He'd eventually become the starter for the Giants, then for the Arizona Cardinals—a franchise that once lived in St. Louis. All Warner did was lead the Cardinals out of the desert and into their first Super Bowl in the 2009 game.

Along the way, the devout Warner met and married Brenda Meonio, a single mother of two, one a boy named Zach who sustained a brain injury as an infant. Warner adopted those children, and with Brenda had five more. The family has performed endless work for a variety of causes through Warner's foundation.

"It's been an amazing ride," Warner said upon his retirement in 2010. "I don't think I could have dreamt it would have played out like it has, but I've been humbled every day that I woke up the last 12 years and amazed that God would choose to use me to do what he's given me the opportunity to do."

Super Bowl XXXV

In 2000, Ray Lewis made all the wrong kinds of headlines, and he wasn't even in the Super Bowl. A year later, he was the game's MVP.

Baltimore's All-Pro linebacker will forever be remembered for both of the NFL championships he helped the Ravens win. He also will always carry a stigma from whatever involvement he had at a murder scene in Atlanta after the first Super Bowl of the millennium.

Two of Lewis's friends were killed, and he eventually pled guilty to obstruction of justice after being charged with two counts of murder, counts that were dropped. Details of the incident have remained murky and the murders unsolved. Lewis remained free by making a deal with prosecutors in exchange for his testimony concerning two companions that night—neither of whom was convicted of the crimes.

At one point, though, Lewis spent a night in jail; later, his young son Ray III would ask his father why he was on television wearing an orange jumpsuit and handcuffs. So his role in the stabbings outside a nightclub, however large or small it was, became as much a topic for Super Bowl XXXV in Tampa as was how Lewis and Baltimore's shutdown defense would handle the New York Giants.

"It was never about those two kids lying dead in the street," Lewis said. "It was about Ray Lewis, and that's not right. Don't be mad at me because I'm at center stage." Then Lewis attempted to shove aside the storyline the way he shoved ball carriers to the ground. "I hear your questions," he said, "and it's my prerogative not to answer them. That chapter is closed."

Not really—then or years later.

The 35th chapter of the Super Bowl, however, would be written by Lewis and his cohorts, who had put together performances reminiscent of the Steel Curtain and Monsters of the Midway. No nickname necessary for these Ravens, though.

"Nah," Lewis said. "We're the 2000 Baltimore Ravens, and that's enough."

More than enough for the Giants. Lewis keyed a unit that allowed 66 yards rushing, 86 net passing (with four sacks), and no points in a 34–7 romp. New York's only score came on Ron Dixon's 97-yard kickoff return, which was sandwiched by Duane Starks's 49-yard runback of an interception for a TD and Jermaine Lewis's 84-yard kickoff return to the end zone. Yep, three touchdowns in 36 seconds, none scored by an offense.

It never really was a close game, with Giants quarterback Kerry Collins besieged by the relentless Ravens. Lewis didn't have overwhelming stats with three solo tackles and four blocked passes, but he was the leader of a unit that decided the game—and nearly every game in Baltimore's championship run.

"I told Shannon Sharpe and I told Jamal Lewis: Give us 10 points and the game is over," Lewis said. "That's not boasting. If you give us 10 points, game over. You go down against our defense, you're in a whole lot of trouble. We've dominated people like that all year. And they didn't score on us. Make sure you quote that. They didn't score on our defense."

Yet it was quarterback Trent Dilfer who was invited to Disney World, not Lewis. And it was tight end Sharpe and four other Ravens who wound up on a Wheaties box.

Lewis never publicly expressed any discontent about not reaping the rewards most Super Bowl heroes get. Then again, he claimed there was a much higher personal reward for him.

"To be where I was last year and to hear everyone say that it's going to affect me, I had a higher power that said everything's going to be all right," he said. "And that's why I'm here right now. If you put this in a storybook, nobody would believe it.

"If the world wants to see me stumble now, I'll stumble with a [Super Bowl] ring on my finger."

Super Bowl XXXVI

When the New England Patriots showed up in New Orleans to meet the Greatest Show on Turf in Super Bowl XXXVI, they were 14-point underdogs. With a second-year quarterback, a so-so offense, and plenty of luck, the Patriots had won the AFC, which certainly didn't impress the oddsmakers in Las Vegas.

The game was expected to be so much of a rout that more attention was paid to the planned halftime show featuring U2 remembering the victims of the September 11 terrorist attacks on New York and Washington. Bono and the boys absolutely delivered with the most memorable and moving halftime performance the Super Bowl has ever seen.

Then Tom Brady, Ty Law, Adam Vinatieri, and the Patriots delivered, too.

"We came to win a football game," Brady said, "and we didn't plan on leaving as losers."

Few people outside of Foxboro, Massachusetts, saw that coming. While the Rams had the powerhouse offense led by QB Kurt Warner, who won his second league MVP trophy, do-it-all running back Marshall Faulk, and standout receivers Isaac Bruce and Torry Holt, New England had, well, no one was really sure.

Except for good fortune. Everyone knew that.

In Game 2 of the schedule, first-string quarterback Drew Bledsoe was lost with a chest injury against the Jets. In stepped an untested Brady, who in college at Michigan had struggled to keep his starting position, then slipped to 199th in the 2000 draft.

Brady played well enough to keep the Patriots in contention, but barely, with a 5-5 record. Then, even as Bledsoe returned to health, Brady kept the job, and the Patriots went on a six-game winning streak to capture the AFC East.

Still, the Patriots appeared doomed in the snow against the Raiders in the divisional playoff round before good luck—and an obscure rule that since has been changed—rescued them.

Oakland led 13–10 but couldn't run out the clock and New England got the ball with 2:06 remaining. Looking like a seasoned veteran—something he would repeat in the Super Bowl (and hundreds of other times)—Brady marched his team downfield on the slippery white turf.

Then he was sacked by star defensive back Charles Woodson and lost the ball. Oakland recovered. "I thought it was over and I started walking out there," said Patriots linebacker Tedy Bruschi. "I thought that our season was coming to an end."

So did much of the football world. But the replay buzzer sounded on referee Walt Coleman's belt, and he headed to the video monitor. What he saw was the tuck rule in action.

"The [video replay] shot . . . was from the front, which gave me a clear look at exactly what happened on the play," Coleman said. "And what it showed is Brady's arm's coming forward. And Woodson hits him and the ball falls out of his hand. And that's clearly an incomplete forward pass. It was easy."

It was easily the most controversial call of the season, among the most contentious in any season. New England kept the ball, and despite three or so inches of snow on the ground, dead-eye Adam Vinatieri tied it with a field goal. Then he won the game in overtime with another kick.

"Just looking at their facial expressions, you just saw guys that were deflated," Patriots guard Damien Woody said of the Raiders. "They just didn't know how to take the call. You knew from that point forward we were going to win that football game, just off their body language."

After, uh, tucking away that victory, winning the AFC title at Pittsburgh wasn't such a challenge, even though Brady missed it with a sprained ankle and Bledsoe returned to the lineup.

And so it was on to the Superdome, which The Associated Press described as "a site that resembled a military fortress as much as a stadium."

Fans were told to show up as much as five hours before kickoff to get through the unprecedented security.

The game had been pushed back one week because the NFL postponed Week 2 games after the terrorist attacks. There was no break between the conference championships and the Super Bowl. That seemed to work in the Rams' favor because Bill Belichick and the Patriots' coaching staff wouldn't have an extra week to design a defensive game plan to slow St. Louis, which scored 503 points, 94 more than the next most prolific team.

Belichick's marching orders for his defense became clear from the outset: smash-mouth football.

"Yeah, we were challenging those guys all game," cornerback Law said. "We were getting up in their face. You have to do that.

"They say it's the best track team in the National Football League, but I never saw anybody win a 100-yard dash with someone standing in front of them."

Or knocking the stuffing out of them.

New England took advantage of some lax officiating, and regulations that allowed defensive backs like Law to be superaggressive, more free with their hands than now is allowed after several rules changes. Law ran back an interception 47 yards for the Patriots' first touchdown. Terrell Buckley scooted 15 yards with a fumble recovery to set up another TD. Otis Smith returned another interception 30 yards, leading to a field goal.

The Rams were reeling, down 17–3 late in the third quarter. "We didn't have any choice," Warner said. "We had to get going."

Instead, New England's Tebucky Jones got going in the opposite direction, covering 98 yards with Warner's fumble. But the serendipity that accompanied the Patriots on the tuck play against Oakland turned on them; a holding call negated the return.

Warner sneaked for a 2-yard touchdown, his first on the ground all season, to make it 17–10.

St. Louis got the ball back and, at last, was looking like an offensive juggernaut, covering 55 yards in three plays and 21 seconds. Ricky Proehl's 26-yard reception tied it.

Ninety seconds remained.

"We had a lot of new life," Warner said. "We figured we'd hold them and have overtime." Seemed logical with an inexperienced quarterback running the other team, and with all the momentum in the Rams' favor.

Belichick and Brady, in what would become a preview of their attacking approach through the years, had other thoughts. As the AP reported: "I was planning to go out there and win the game," said Brady, who was so calm he took a nap in the locker room before the game. "Adam wasn't going to miss that kick."

Stunning the 72,922 in attendance—not to mention the Rams— New England went for the jugular. Brady guided the Patriots 53 yards, the key play a 23-yard completion to Troy Brown. Out trotted Vinatieri, and on the last play of regulation, he nailed a 48-yarder, giving it some extra body language as it soared through the uprights.

It was the second-biggest upset in Super Bowl history, behind only the Jets' shocker over Baltimore in 1969. "We've got a whole team full of underdogs," Brady said. "And now we're the top dogs."

On a day filled with tributes to America and Americans who serve the nation in all capacities, it seemed fitting that the champions were called Patriots.

Super Bowl XXXVII

THE UNIMAGINABLE HAD HAPPENED: THE LAUGHINGSTOCK OF THE NFL was doing the laughing.

No franchise had been more ridiculed, more dismissed, more ignored even, than the Tampa Bay Buccaneers. From their early uniforms, a garish orange with a winking pirate who wouldn't scare a goldfish, to their penchant for losing lots of games every season, the Bucs were the pits. So bad that Bo Jackson, their top overall draft choice in 1986, played baseball rather than sign with them.

Ah, but these Bucs were scoundrels of a different sort. For one, they'd ditched the awful jersey for something more befitting football: pewter and red and black, with crossed swords and a skull on the helmet.

For another, they were winners. And yes, these Bucs had a Jackson, too: Dexter, a safety who, while not nearly in Bo's class as a player, knew something about winning.

Jackson had two interceptions as Tampa's terrific defense shut down Oakland's prolific offense led by league MVP Rich Gannon. In all, the Bucs had five sacks and five interceptions.

"When you have a defense like we do," Jackson said, "it's just a matter of time until we make the plays. When I first came to the team I knew they had some great players like the Sapps, the Lynches and the Brookses. These guys came from nothing and came together as a championship caliber team."

The real reason the Bucs overcame their wretched history was coaching. Two coaches in particular: Tony Dungy and Jon Gruden.

Dungy instilled every principle that goes into winning—and that the franchise lacked for decades—when he took over in 1996. Tampa had a

13-year string of losing records and a poisoned environment marked by underachieving, laziness, and ineptitude nearly everywhere. GM Rich McKay—whose dad, John, was the team's first coach and famously, when asked about his winless Bucs' execution, cracked, "I'm in favor of it"—recognized the dire need for change.

McKay turned to Dungy, who learned the coaching craft with the Chuck Noll Steelers. Together they built through the draft, through the nurturing of youngsters, and through wise acquisitions of veterans. One problem: Dungy couldn't get the Bucs to the Super Bowl. They came close, holding "The Greatest Show on Turf" Rams to 11 points in falling in the 1999 NFC title contest.

But despite no losing records in his tenure, team owners fired Dungy and made the kind of marauding charge for Gruden that would make Captain Jack Sparrow proud. Sensing their first choice, Steve Mariucci, would not leave the 49ers, they called Raiders owner Al Davis to seek permission to talk to Gruden, who was under contract in Oakland. In turn sensing an opportunity to, well, extort the Bucs in return for a coach Davis felt had grabbed too much freedom, the asking price became first- and second-round draft picks in 2002, a No. 1 in 2003, and a No. 2 in 2004, plus $8 million in cash.

The Bucs bit, then signed Gruden to a five-year, $17.5 million contract.

"I'm not shy. I don't have thin skin," Gruden said. "I'm going to coach with the style that I've always coached with and I welcome any input I can get from ownership."

The input was this: "The vision is what it always has been. And that's to put forward a championship-caliber team," owner Joel Glazer said. "We're always going to push and strive for this organization and this team to be the best in everything it does."

Even on offense, Gruden's strength, Dungy's downfall.

Gruden guided the Bucs to a 12-4 record mostly with Dungy's guys, but with plenty of alterations the new coach made. The Bucs routed San Francisco and Philadelphia to finally reach the big game.

Lo and behold, in their way—in Gruden's way—were Davis's Raiders.

Dwight Smith

Somehow, Dwight Smith did not race off with MVP honors in the 2003 Super Bowl. Having defensive backfield mate Dexter Jackson get them was just fine with him.

Smith picked off two passes, just like Jackson. Smith's timing wasn't quite as good as Jackson's, whose picks had more impact on the 48–21 final score, both coming in the first half. But Smith took both of his interceptions to the end zone, scoring on returns of 44 yards in the third quarter to make it 34–3, and 50 yards with just 2 seconds on the clock.

The MVP ballots were in and counted when Smith became the only player with a pair of TDs on interception runbacks in a Super Bowl.

"This is the thing I've been doing for 17 years of my life," said Smith, a nickel back and one of the least heralded Bucs defenders. "Play football and make plays was what I was known to do."

Unfortunately, Smith never became known for much more than that stellar performance in San Diego. Soon after the victory, Smith was arrested in Clearwater, Florida, for aggravated assault, charged with brandishing a gun at another motorist. He pled guilty, was fined, placed on one year's probation, and ordered to take anger management classes.

Two years later, he again was arrested and charged with aggravated assault with a weapon after Smith pulled a pellet gun on two men who approached his car at a McDonald's drive-through. Smith did not shoot the gun.

Soon after, Smith was gone: to New Orleans, Minnesota, and Detroit. He was a starter for several of those years, but he never became a star.

Gruden relished the challenge. So did his players, who saw the matchup as the ultimate chance to "shut up the world," according to defensive tackle Warren Sapp. Thanks to Sapp, Derrick Brooks, John Lynch, Jackson, Dwight Smith, and the rest of the powerhouse defense, Gannon and the Raiders never got going.

"Jon Gruden was Gannon," Bucs defensive coordinator Monte Kiffin said, referring to how Gruden designed and nurtured the offense Gannon oversaw. "Nobody can be like Gannon like Gruden can. He taught Gannon. He was in Gannon's head."

Super Bowl XXXVIII-XXXIX

Repeat champions in Super Bowls aren't particularly rare. Or at least they weren't before the turn of the century.

Green Bay won the first two. Miami, Pittsburgh (twice), San Francisco, Dallas, and Denver all did it.

But since the calendar hit the 2000s, only the Patriots have managed the feat. In fact, since New England captured Super Bowls XXXVIII and XXXIX, only Seattle in 2015 got into position for a repeat. And the Patriots knocked them off to ruin that.

The Patriots of the 2003 and '04 seasons probably weren't as good as the 2007 and 2011 teams that lost to the Giants in Super Bowls. Yet they walked off with the crown in wins over Carolina, then over Philadelphia.

Why?

"Everyone steps up," linebacker Tedy Bruschi said. "You don't have to all be stars. You just have to step up when the time comes."

Tom Brady and Deion Branch stepped up the most in these back-to-back triumphs.

Still only 26, Brady wasn't yet the sharp-shooting, no-holds-barred quarterback he would later become. There still were a few restraints placed on Brady by coach Bill Belichick, who was reared on strong defense and special teams and just enough offense as the best formula for winning.

What Brady had was moxie. And no fear of failure. Never did that show more than in his performance at Reliant Stadium in Houston in the 32–29 win over Carolina.

After a dull, feel-'em-out first quarter, the teams combined for 24 points in the final 3:05 of the second period. Brady hit Branch for a TD and David Givens for another, both from 5 yards. Steve Smith caught a

39-yard touchdown pass and John Kasay made a field goal at the halftime gun.

Then things got tight again, with no scoring in the third quarter. Weird? Even Brady felt that—and not because a streaker had run onto the field, or because Janet Jackson had her "costume malfunction" in the halftime show.

"You just felt like both teams were capable of putting up points," he said. "But neither of us could do it."

Then came the final quarter—and 37 more points.

The Panthers grabbed the lead 22–21 with a 90-yard drive—85 came on the longest play from scrimmage in any Super Bowl, a pass from Jake Delhomme to Muhsin Muhammad—after intercepting Brady, but had missed twice going for two-point conversions.

Unfazed, Brady marched New England to another go-ahead score, a 1-yard pass to linebacker Mike Vrabel, who made a habit throughout his career of grabbing touchdown throws from Tom Terrific. Kevin Faulk's run on the conversion—see, Panthers, that is how you get the two points—made it 29–22.

Carolina simply shrugged and used 1:43 to tie it on Ricky Proehl's 12-yard reception. Like the 2002 match with St. Louis, overtime in a Super Bowl loomed for New England. Or, once again, maybe it didn't.

Kasay sailed his kickoff out of bounds, a huge gaffe that gave the Patriots the ball at their 40 yard line with more than a minute left. An eternity for Brady.

"Who would you rather have running a two-minute drive than Tom Brady?" Patriots offensive coordinator Charlie Weis said. "I'll take him 10 times out of 10 times."

With the calm demeanor of someone out for a leisurely Sunday stroll, Brady guided his team 37 yards, and with 4 seconds remaining, Adam Vinatieri almost as calmly nailed a 41-yard field goal.

"Hey, it's Adam," Brady said with a wide smile. "No worries."

Branch actually had a major worry before Super Bowl XXXIX: finding enough tickets.

A native of Albany, Georgia, well within driving distance of Jacksonville, site of the game, Branch got requests from "maybe half of" the

Adam Vinatieri

He has been called the best clutch kicker in NFL history, quite a claim considering all the great legs that have swung through footballs in the pros. It's difficult to argue with that description when it comes to Adam Vinatieri. After all, no one's field goals have been the difference in three Super Bowls, including two he nailed at the end of regulation.

Still going strong for the Indianapolis Colts, with whom he won a championship the very season he left New England, Vinatieri booted the decisive three-pointer from 48 yards for the Patriots in the last seconds to beat St. Louis in 2002, and from 41 yards with :04 on the clock two years later to beat Carolina.

In Super Bowl XXXIX, his chip shot from 22 yards provided the winning points, albeit with 8:40 remaining, in a victory over Philadelphia.

The numbers tell us plenty. So do the honors; consider his three All-Pro selections, including 2014 when he was the league's oldest player. Vinatieri has been a premier placekicker in the NFL for two decades and counting.

But all that doesn't measure the courage and the confidence a player must carry to be able to perform in the most pressurized situations.

"He's as good of a kicker, good of a clutch kicker, and consistent kicker that's probably ever been in the game," New England coach Bill Belichick said. "Mentally, he's as tough as they come in terms of concentration, focus, discipline, blocking out all the things that he can't control and just doing his job.

"Nobody makes all of them. But if you've got to have one kick with everything on the line, he's the one you want kicking it."

whole town. He knew he couldn't fill anywhere close to the demand, helping about 75 get into the stadium.

"A lot of them didn't go to the game," Branch said after earning MVP honors in the 24–21 win against the Eagles. "I didn't have enough tickets."

High praise from someone who rarely hands it out. Of course, Vinatieri is directly responsible for much of the finger jewelry Belichick owns.

Vinatieri had an interesting backstory, though nothing like the one he would tell The Associated Press about his great-great grandfather Felix.

"In 1876, Felix was the bandleader for the 7th Cavalry," AP columnist Jim Litke wrote. "On the day Gen. George Custer prepared his troops to march on Little Big Horn, he ordered Felix Vinatieri and his 16-member brass band to stay behind on a supply steamboat, instead of meeting up with the rest of the unit. On June 26, Custer and 276 of his men were massacred in an epic battle against Crazy Horse and his Sioux warriors."

NFL kickers are a rare sporting breed. Hardly ever are they drafted, and certainly not from a lower-division school. Vinatieri came out of South Dakota State in 1996 and somehow drew the attention of one of the toughest men in football to impress, Bill Parcells. "After he tackled [Herschel] Walker on a kick return," Parcells recalled, "I told the fellas in the locker room, 'That's not just a kicker, that guy is a football player.'"

Vinatieri, a West Point dropout who played in the World League of American Football after graduating college, replaced one of Parcells's all-time "guys," Matt Bahr, in New England. Maybe that was even more challenging than making Super Bowl–clinching kicks.

"It's been a lot of fun," he said. "There have been so many great moments throughout my career. The first time you win the Super Bowl is something you dream about as a kid. The Snow Bowl game [a home playoff win over Oakland in a near blizzard also known as the "Tuck Rule Game"] was fun. Tackling Herschel Walker as a rookie was great fun.

"It's still fun."

He certainly had enough catches: 11 for 133 yards. His receptions tied a record originally set by Jerry Rice and Dan Ross, and eight of his catches were on Patriots scoring drives.

His big-time production, even though he didn't get into the end zone, outdid the work of the more-heralded Terrell Owens for Philly.

Owens, always looking for headlines while Branch performed under the radar, returned from a broken leg and had nine receptions for 122 yards.

"They say big players step up in big games," Branch said. "All the hoopla was about T.O. He's a great player. He really sucked it up tonight. But I want to show I have the same type of talent as those guys."

Branch was coming off an injury-shortened season; a knee problem limited him to nine games and just 35 catches. He told The Associated Press that he was "so frustrated during the recovery" that he didn't travel to every road game.

"My teammates kept pushing me to get better," he said. "They were telling me, 'We're going to need you soon.' I'm just thankful they didn't put me on IR."

Branch and Brady put Philly on the wrong end of the score, tearing apart a zone defense that had humbled many other opponents. "He's a very dynamic player," Brady said. "He can do it all—getting open, doing great things after he caught the ball."

Unlike Brady, Branch never did great things the rest of his career, making a move to Seattle as a free agent in 2006 that never paid off. But he was a key element in New England joining Dallas as the only franchise to win three Super Bowls in four seasons.

Why were the Patriots so successful in that span? Try experience and resolve. Not very heroic terms, eh? Perhaps not individually. When 53 players master those traits, it provides something special.

"To me this trophy belongs to these players," Belichick said after the 2005 Super Bowl. "They met all comers this year, a very challenging year. We started at the bottom of the mountain like everybody else, and we're thrilled to get to the top. It was one fight against 31 other teams to try to win this Super Bowl and win that trophy. We're happy that we did it. And I'll leave the comparisons and historical perspectives to everybody else."

Despite such protestations, the word *dynasty* began being thrown around after the victory in Jacksonville. "When you're in the middle of it, you're not thinking about what you're doing," Weis said. "Dynasties are talked about 10 years later."

And surely well beyond that.

Super Bowl XL

You could paint this Super Bowl black and gold. How fitting, with the Rolling Stones playing at halftime, that the Pittsburgh Steelers would win Super Bowl XL. And pretty much right down the road in Detroit, an easy drive for Steelers Nation, especially compared to where fans of the opponent, the Seattle Seahawks, had to trek from.

Even better was the overriding story of this game: The Bus Comes Home.

Then the Bus left with the Lombardi Trophy.

Since joining the Steelers in a trade with the Rams in 1996, Jerome Bettis, a future Hall of Fame running back, had mowed down the opposition while becoming one of the true leaders on the Steelers. His philosophy was simple: "Climb aboard the Bus and let's get where we are headed."

Bettis rushed for more than 1,000 yards in six straight seasons. At 5'11", 252 pounds, he was a load near the goal line, scoring 78 times for the Steelers.

But each of his nine previous seasons in Pittsburgh ended prematurely. No AFC titles. No championship glory. And late in the 2005 schedule, with the Steelers at 7-5, it didn't look likely that the final ride for the Bus could end up in his hometown playing in the Super Bowl.

Bettis wasn't even a major cog for the Steelers that season, a role player used mostly in short-yardage situations. Sure, he had nine TDs rushing, but he had only 110 rushing attempts, by far the fewest in his career, as Willie Parker took over the primary tailback job.

Bettis had been considering retirement throughout the season. With their playoff chances collapsing, the Steelers gathered for a team meeting. Each player, including Bettis, asked the others to rededicate themselves.

"It was, 'Let's just go out there and play Steelers Football,'" Bettis said. And they did, winning their final four games to earn a wild-card playoff berth, yielding a total of 33 points in those victories.

On the road they went in January, winning at Cincinnati, the AFC Central winner. Then they stunned the top-seeded Colts at Indianapolis.

When the Steelers went into Denver and tamed the Broncos, they were Super Bowl bound. Bettis was like every other member of the roster: No one had been that far in his career.

"I promised Jerome last year that I would get him here," said Ben Roethlisberger, whose poor performance in the previous season's AFC championship game led to a loss to New England. "I didn't promise him I would win it.

"Then after the Cincinnati game, I promised him I would get him four game balls." Bettis was one game ball short. He also knew it would be his last shot at a game ball: Retirement was next on his agenda.

A few days after the Denver win, he told Steelers ownership what was ahead. No one was surprised. "I let them know this was it," Bettis said. "It was probably going to be my last game, either way. My body's been breaking down. I didn't want to talk to Bill Cowher and distract him from preparation. Still, he knew this was the last ride."

What a ride it would be. Bettis's family entertained his teammates for a home-cooked dinner. He hosted a bowling tournament—Bettis is a member of that sport's Hall of Fame, too. He received a key to the city. And he made sure the team from the Steel City got the most out of its stay in the Motor City.

"It means a lot, especially to my mom and dad, who want to be as hospitable as they can, being that this is home for me," he said while wearing a Detroit Tigers hat and a jacket with "Detroit" across the chest.

Even with all of those celebrations, preparation remained a focal point for the Bus and his riders, uh, teammates. Most notably, Hines Ward.

A do-everything player at Georgia who even had a stint as a quarterback, Ward had settled in as a Steeler at wide receiver. Eventually, he would become the franchise's career receptions king, quite an achievement considering that Canton members Lynn Swann and John Stallworth played in Pittsburgh.

On this February Sunday, inside the comforts of Ford Field—which could have easily been mistaken for Heinz Field considering all the Terrible Towels waving in the stands—Bettis would lead the Steelers onto the field in pregame introductions. Ward would lead them on the field during the game.

"Joey Porter said, 'You lead us out there,' so I did," Bettis said. "They gave me a moment I'll never forget."

Ward gave him and all Steelers fans several such moments. He caught five passes for 123 yards. He had one run for 18 yards. And with the Seahawks having closed to 14–10, Ward got free to catch a halfback option throw from Antwaan Randle El—another former college QB—to clinch it.

Among his first thoughts: what it all meant for Bettis.

"I didn't want Jerome to go out like that," Ward recalled of the previous year's loss to the Patriots. "For him to come so close and fall short of the Super Bowl last year, I took it very hard. It's not often you play with a Hall of Fame running back or Hall of Fame guy, period. And having him come back, winning the Super Bowl from where it all started, it's a fairy tale come true."

As for Bettis, well, the Bus would now be parked.

"This is why I started 13 years ago, on this quest," Bettis said. "Along the way, I amassed a lot of yards and a lot of Pro Bowls, but none of that was significant because it wasn't the team goals. The team goal has always been to win a championship, and now I have a championship.

"Mission accomplished."

Super Bowl XLI

It rained on the Super Bowl for the first time.

Peyton Manning and Tony Dungy barely noticed. The journey to Dolphin Stadium had been a circuitous one for both the quarterback and his coach. In many ways, just getting there was a historic achievement.

The first family of quarterbacking had yet to taste NFL championship glory when Manning led the Colts into Super Bowl XLI. Peyton's dad, Archie, was one of the greatest of college quarterbacks, a legend at Ole Miss. But while Archie survived with awful teams throughout his 13-year pro career in New Orleans, Houston, and Minnesota, he never sniffed the playoffs, let alone the big payoff.

Peyton, the top overall pick in the 1998 draft, already had earned two of what would become a record five MVP awards, but his lack of success in the postseason offset those individual honors.

Dungy turned around the NFL's most inept franchise, the Tampa Bay Buccaneers, but was fired in 2001 after failing to get to the big game, unable to build a complementary offense to the Bucs' powerful defense. The next season, under Jon Gruden, Tampa was champion.

Dungy quickly had found a landing spot in Indianapolis, and this time he had an offense, guided by the most prepared and, perhaps, the most intelligent quarterback in NFL history.

So when Manning led the Colts back from an 18-point hole in the AFC championship game against archrival New England, then on a decisive 80-yard drive late in the fourth quarter, well, as Dave Goldberg wrote for The Associated Press: "The demons can relocate to some other team's locker room. Peyton Manning and Tony Dungy are Super Bowl material now."

For Manning, there was only annoyance when asked if the weight of previous failures had been lifted. "I don't get into monkeys and vindication," he said. "I don't play that card. I know how hard I worked this season, I know how hard I worked this week."

Dungy was more emotional, but not necessarily because he'd gotten over a personal coaching hump. You see, the coach on the other sideline for the Super Bowl would be his former assistant, his friend Lovie Smith of the Bears. Both Dungy and Smith are African Americans. No black head coaches had ever worked a Super Bowl. "It means a lot," Dungy said. "I'm very proud to be representing African Americans. I'm very proud of Lovie."

Then it was time to beat Lovie and the Bears, and things didn't start out too well for Indy. Chicago's devastating kick returner, Devin Hester, ran back the opening kickoff 92 yards for a touchdown with 14 seconds gone. Before he'd even taken a snap, Manning was down seven points. Combine that with the nasty weather—remember, the Colts play their home games indoors—and conditions were not ideal for Indy.

Then Manning hit Reggie Wayne for a 53-yard score. And by half-time, when Prince performed "Purple Rain" in between the Miami droplets, the Colts were on top 16–14.

They led 22–17 when the defense, Dungy's specialty, salted away the title. Kelvin Hayden stole Rex Grossman's pass and sped 56 yards to the end zone in the fourth quarter. The Bears were done.

While Manning wasn't spectacular, his 25-for-38 performance for 247 yards and his overall command of his team and the situation earned him the MVP trophy. No more non-winner tag, even if it really never applied.

"If people thought that, well, that's just wrong," Dungy said. "But now he's done it. He's a Hall of Fame quarterback, one of the best that's ever played the game. And he's a Super Bowl champion."

As was Dungy, in a historic way, too.

"I tell you what, I'm proud to be representing African-American coaches, to be the first African-American coach to win this," Dungy said. "It means an awful lot to our country. But again, more than anything, I said it before, Lovie Smith and I, not only the first two African

Americans, but Christian coaches showing you can win doing it the Lord's way. We're more proud of that."

For both Manning and Dungy, it was the pinnacle of their time together. Dungy would retire after two more seasons and no more Super Bowl trips. Manning would get to the title contest three more times, once with Indy and twice with Denver, losing twice and then finally winning in Super Bowl 50 following the 2015 season.

They would always have Miami. "The disappointment you have along the way," Dungy said, "it helps you appreciate it more after you finally do achieve it."

Super Bowl XLII

FEW ATHLETES CAST A LONGER SHADOW THEN PEYTON MANNING. Imagine, then, being his kid brother. And playing the same position. And then following Peyton to the Super Bowl, trying to repeat his victory and MVP honors of the previous year. Throw in facing a team obsessed with perfection and Eli Manning's challenge seemed insurmountable.

Except that he's a Manning, which means the higher the obstacle, the more he relishes clearing it. Remember, Eli chose to attend the University of Mississippi, where his father, Archie, was a legend and Hall of Famer. Not even Peyton traveled that road, playing at Tennessee instead.

Yes, Eli already had cleared several hurdles, from childhood to the pros, even managing to alienate some segments of fandom along the way. Chargers fans still rue his decision to power-play his way out of San Diego at the 2004 draft, and soon Patriots diehards would consider him Public Enemy No. 10.

With two older brothers who starred at his high school—eldest sibling Cooper was a receiver who had to quit college ball after his freshman season at Ole Miss because of spinal stenosis—Manning learned young the value of quietly but efficiently going about chasing your goals.

"I always thought they enjoyed being around me," Eli once said of his brothers. "They were babysitting me a lot of times. Then I found out they had been grounded and that's why."

Eli recalled as a kid being tortured by Peyton: "He would pin me down and take his knuckles and knock on my chest and make me name the 12 schools in the SEC. I didn't know them all at the time, but I quickly learned them. . . . I don't suggest anyone else try it out, but it definitely made me learn the schools of the SEC. Once I figured those out, he moved on.

"There were 28 teams in the NFL at that point, so all teams in the NFL. I had to get my studying on for that. Then once I figured that out, the one I never got was the 10 brands of cigarettes. When he really wanted to torture me and knew I had no shot of ever getting it, that's when I just started screaming for my mom or dad to come save me."

By 2007, Manning had established himself as a quality NFL quarterback. No, not on the level of Peyton, or of Eli's rival in Super Bowl XLII, Tom Brady. Eli was no superstar, and his inconsistent performances at times had folks in the Big Apple questioning his staying power.

Then Manning took that next step, from re*li*able to *eli*te.

He guided the Giants to playoff road victories at Tampa, Dallas, and over Green Bay in frigid Lambeau Field. He'd become a difference maker.

The issue at hand, though, was to make that final leap, over Brady and the 18-0 Patriots, who'd beaten New York in the regular-season finale.

Manning noted that the Giants drew some confidence from testing New England in that defeat, and that the roll they were on had boosted their faith even more. And when they drove 63 yards in nearly 10 minutes, running off 16 plays before kicking a field goal, he said the Giants "knew we could do this."

Still, it would take plenty of heroics against the record-setting Brady and receiver Randy Moss. It would take a fierce pass rush, which New York used to make Brady uncomfortable and to neutralize Moss. It would take efficiency with the ball, and patience to put together time-consuming drives.

But even after Manning hit David Tyree with a 5-yard pass for a 10–7 fourth-quarter lead, there was a sense throughout the building that New England would find its footing, make the key plays.

When Brady hit Moss for a 6-yard score with 2:32 remaining, that perfect season seemed secure.

Manning thought otherwise: "That's a position you want to be in. You want to have the ball in your hands . . . down, where you've got to score a touchdown."

David Tyree

The litany of improbable Super Bowl heroes stretches through the decades. Finding one who was less likely to grab the spotlight than David Tyree is virtually impossible.

A special teams standout but an afterthought as a receiver, Tyree made all of four regular-season receptions in 2007. With Plaxico Burress, Amani Toomer, Steve Smith, and tight end Jeremy Shockey among Eli Manning's targets, Tyree rarely saw the field as a wideout.

But he was front and center as the Giants mounted a final attempt to spoil the Patriots' perfect season.

Faced with a third-and-5 from the New York 44, Manning was pressured so hard he had to duck away from pass rusher Jarvis Green. Instead of going down, Manning escaped and threw up a prayer.

"It was just kind of like playing backyard football, living in the moment," Tyree said. "Eli's doing his best impression of Michael Vick or something and playing way above the Xs and Os."

Tyree then soared way above defender Rodney Harrison, one of the best safeties in football and, under normal circumstances, a mismatch for a fourth-stringer. Not on this day. Not with a chance for Tyree to secure his place in Super Bowl lore.

Briefly, but just long enough to get some leverage, Tyree pinned the ball against his helmet with his right hand. Then he protected it with his left hand as Harrison tried to snatch it. They both fell awkwardly to the turf, with Tyree cradling the football.

The "helmet catch" was good for 32 yards with less than a minute remaining. Soon after, Burress was in the end zone with the winning touchdown pass, and New England's perfect record had been shattered.

"I don't know that there's ever been a bigger play in the Super Bowl than that play," Giants coach Tom Coughlin said of Tyree's miracle.

"The Catch" forever became a part of Giants legend.

"I am a man that really has to capitalize on his few opportunities," said Tyree, who never caught another pass for the Giants and was out of football after the 2009 season. "Some things just don't make sense and I guess you can just put that catch there with them."

Calmly, with the wisdom of a quarterback far more experienced—such as Peyton, of course—Eli Manning marched his 12-point underdog team downfield. The Giants needed a fourth-and-1 conversion by Brandon Jacobs, and even a scramble by the not-so-nimble Manning.

They also needed a miracle—Tyree's one-handed, against-the-helmet grab of Manning's third-down heave (see sidebar). The catch was made possible when Manning's almost-nimble footwork avoided a near-certain sack by Jarvis Green.

"Yeah," Manning admitted with a smile, "you don't see me do that too much."

What everyone had seen was Manning produce in the most difficult of circumstances. He needed to do so two more times: a 12-yarder to Steve Smith on third-and-11, then, from the 13, hitting a wide-open Plaxico Burress in the left corner of the end zone after defensive back Ellis Hobbs went for a fake toward the goalpost.

Touchdown, with 35 seconds left.

Upset.

In a luxury box at University of Phoenix Stadium, Peyton Manning leaped up, pumping his fist. Younger brother had his ring, too.

Super Bowl XLIII

IT WAS THE PERFECT PASS AT THE PERFECT TIME BY BEN ROETHLIS-
berger. And the catch—what's beyond perfection?

Pittsburgh Steelers fans are so known for their loyalty to the Black
and Gold that it's virtually a sin in Western Pennsylvania to not possess
a Terrible Towel. So when Roethlisberger and Santonio Holmes combined on a play you might draw up in the dirt on the sandlot to beat
Arizona 27–23, folks along all three rivers that meet in the Steel City
were proclaiming it the second-greatest reception since the forward pass
was invented.

Yes, Immaculate Reception II.

In reality, Holmes's masterful work was, by far, the highlight of a
checkered career. His self-described "Tone Time" was marred by off-field
troubles and locker room discord he often sparked—he feuded with his
quarterback with the Jets, Mark Sanchez, and an argument with tackle
Wayne Hunter in the huddle got Holmes benched for the rest of a game.
Not to mention a big contract he couldn't live up to.

But at Raymond James Stadium in Tampa against the surprising and
spunky Cardinals, it was, indeed, Tone Time. "I said that I wanted to be
the guy to make the plays for this team," Holmes said. "Great players step
up in big-time games to make plays."

Holmes already was having a strong game with five receptions.
He'd helped Pittsburgh build a 20–7 lead through three quarters. But
when the Cardinals' Larry Fitzgerald, the more-heralded wideout in this
matchup, showed his All-Pro skills with two TD catches, Arizona surged
on top with 2:37 remaining.

James Harrison

As fearsome as a linebacker could be, James Harrison earned his 2008 NFL Defensive Player of the Year award by running over and through opponents. Had it not been for the late-game heroics of Steelers receiver Santonio Holmes, Harrison might have added Super Bowl MVP to that honor. He would have done so in a most uncommon way.

Harrison made like a slippery halfback in the open field, side-stepping or jumping over would-be tacklers, cutting back and forth—meandering, really—on a 100-yard interception for a touchdown. Had the end zone been another yard further, the exhausted Harrison might not have gotten there.

"Those last couple of yards were probably tougher than anything I've done in my life, but probably more gratifying than anything I've done in football," Harrison said after the longest play in Super Bowl history ended the first half. Instead of pulling ahead 14–10, Arizona was down 17–7.

Harrison surprised Cardinals quarterback Kurt Warner by not rushing on the play from the 1 yard line. He dropped directly in front of receiver Anquan Boldin, and Warner never saw him.

Warner did see Harrison take off down the right sideline with the pick and avoid nearly every Cardinal on the field at the time. Some Steelers, too. "I was seeing jerseys that were friendly and jerseys that weren't," Harrison said.

As his fellow Steelers rushed to the end zone to congratulate Harrison, he remained on his back, unable to summon the energy to rise, the ball lying just as limply at his side on the end line. "To be honest, I really didn't think I'd make it all the way back," Harrison said. "My teammates threw some vicious blocks."

When he finally stood up, Harrison went to the Steelers sideline and put on an oxygen mask while officials replayed his run to make sure he'd scored. Soon, referee Terry McAulay confirmed the touchdown.

Harrison admitted he needed the long halftime break. Appropriately, Bruce Springsteen sang "Born To Run" and "Glory Days" during his halftime show.

Having finally caught his breath, Harrison could only smile about the Boss's choices.

From the sideline, Holmes had seen Fitzgerald's brilliant 64-yard breakaway score to lift Arizona into a 23–20 lead. Now, he thought, it was his turn.

"I dared the team," said Holmes, who'd overcome a rugged childhood—he admitted to once selling drugs while a kid in Florida—to star at Ohio State before being drafted in the first round by Pittsburgh in 2006. "Just give me the ball, give me the chance to make plays and I will do it for you."

Then he did, with three catches to help the Steelers march 72 yards. But they still weren't in the end zone, and on Roethlisberger's next pass, the ball sailed through Holmes's hands.

So Pittsburgh looked elsewhere.

"The first read was the running back in the flat, but he wasn't open," Roethlisberger said. "Then I was going to try to bang it to Hines [Ward], but someone was closing in on it and I was a little nervous about it. It wouldn't have been a touchdown.

"I looked back, scrambled a little bit and saw 'Tone' in the corner. I tried to throw it high so he was going to catch it, or no one was."

When Roethlisberger said corner, he meant the very tightest spot in the back right of the end zone. Plus, throwing the ball high wasn't necessarily the right place to hit Holmes, who was a little under 5-foot-10.

When Roethlisberger let go of the ball as Holmes headed to the corner, three Cardinals defenders were in the area. Two were in close coverage of Holmes. Yet, the ball found his outstretched hands as he leaped. When Holmes came down, he cradled the ball and, seemingly beyond the rules of physics, got both feet—tippy-toes actually—in bounds.

Just before his teammates stormed on top of him, Holmes could be seen with his legs outstretched on the turf and the ball safely tucked in his arms. Then he disappeared in a pileup of Pittsburgh pleasure.

"What he did tonight was similar to what he did in the month of January in the playoffs to get to this game," coach Mike Tomlin said. "In big moments we know what we can get from him."

Unfortunately, that was about the last big moment from Holmes. He soon wore out his welcome in Pittsburgh, and then with the Jets. Five years after his Super Bowl star turn, Holmes was a journeyman searching for an NFL job.

The 2010s

Super Bowl XLIV

It would be a massive overstatement to say Drew Brees coming to New Orleans was a critical step in the healing and rebuilding of New Orleans after Hurricane Katrina devastated Bayou Country.

Then again, it might be a spot-on observation.

The horror that was Katrina in 2005 was felt throughout the region. One of the binding forces in the restoration and revival of the area was sports. Specifically, football. Even more specifically, the Saints.

Forced to become a bunch of nomads when the Louisiana Superdome was severely damaged by the storm, the Saints played home games in Baton Rouge, San Antonio, and even one at the New Jersey Meadowlands—against the Giants, no less. It was farcical, and fears that owner Tom Benson would permanently move the team out of the Big Easy made everyone in New Orleans uneasy.

Then, under mighty pressure from NFL commissioner Paul Tagliabue and other franchise owners to have the Saints return to New Orleans, Benson brought the team back and hired Sean Payton as coach.

Among Payton's first moves was signing a free agent quarterback with a damaged shoulder: Brees.

Almost immediately, Brees became more than an elite player who would guide the Saints to previously unattained heights and set an assortment of passing records on the way. He became a fixture in the community's efforts to reconstruct itself, to revitalize "Nawlins." Brees worked to restore child care projects and facilities in New Orleans through his Brees Dream Foundation. He led anti-bullying campaigns and cancer research fundraisers.

For those efforts, which came naturally to him, Brees won the 2006 Walter Payton Award as the NFL's Man of the Year, sharing it with San Diego's LaDainian Tomlinson. Yes, Brees became a hero off the field long before he guided the Saints to their first Super Bowl in 2010.

"I've had people tell me they'd never let their child get a jersey for anybody that they didn't think was a good role model, no matter how good a player they were," Brees told The Associated Press. "But they would allow their child to get a Drew Brees jersey because they felt like I was that type of person for their child and that's probably the highest compliment you can be paid by a parent."

Clearly, Brees did not need to solidify his standing in Bayou Country, but if he could bring home the Saints' first NFL crown—and beat New Orleans native Peyton Manning and the Colts in the process—well, he just might have been knighted.

But things didn't start well for the Saints at Miami.

Indianapolis grabbed a 10–0 lead through the first quarter and was ahead 10–6 at halftime. New Orleans's high-powered attack was pedestrian, and the Saints needed a serious spark heading into the second half.

It came thanks to some derring-do: Payton called for an onside kick to open the third period. New Orleans recovered, leading to Brees's 16-yard TD toss to Pierre Thomas. The Saints led for the first time.

They soon fell behind again—Manning was on the other side, remember. But Brees simply shrugged and guided the Saints to a field goal, and then the decisive march for a touchdown: a 2-yard pass to Jeremy Shockey. For good measure, Brees hit Lance Moore for a two-point conversion.

The Saints were less than six minutes from the championship. But Manning had the ball.

Moments later, Saints defensive back Tracy Porter had the ball, cradling it in his arm as he sped to the end zone for a 74-yard interception return touchdown and the final margin.

Choosing this Super Bowl hero was no big chore: Brees had gone 32 for 39 for 288 yards and two touchdowns. His passer rating was 114.5. His popularity rating was off the charts.

Despite Manning's Big Easy roots, there was no question where the city's loyalties lay. Brees was New Orleans's guy; the Saints were its team.

And the celebrations Brees made possible were as wild as any Mardi Gras festivities.

"Our victory last night was the culmination of four years of hard work, fighting through a lot of adversity, ups and downs and more importantly than that, representing a city that has been through so much," Brees said hours after the 31–17 win. "Along the way, people have asked me so many times, 'Do you look at it as a burden or extra pressure? Do you feel like you're carrying the weight of the city on your team's shoulders?'

"I said, 'No, not at all. We look at it as a responsibility.' Our city, our fans, gave us strength and we owe this to them. . . . There's no people that you would want to win for more than the city of New Orleans."

Super Bowl XLV

Aaron Rodgers knows all about waiting your turn.

Unfortunately for Rodgers, Packers fans are a bit more spoiled.

After all, which franchise won the first two Super Bowls? Green Bay was already dubbed "Titletown USA" before the AFL and NFL first faced off for the championship spoils. Beating the Chiefs and Raiders back in the 1960s only solidified that title entitlement the Cheeseheads felt.

Then the Packers went nearly three decades before Brett Favre guided them back to the top. And by the 2010 season, the Lambeau faithful once more were mighty antsy about ending another championship drought.

That these Packers were the team to do it was questionable. They had gone 10-6, needing to win their final two regular-season contests just to make the playoffs. Then, with Rodgers unstoppable, came wins at Philadelphia, Atlanta, and archrival Chicago to get to the first Super Bowl hosted by the Dallas metroplex, where vicious winter storms plagued the entire week of buildup to the game, but suited both sides just fine.

In a classic matchup with Pittsburgh—Cheeseheads vs. Terrible Towels—the Steelers seemed to have most of the edges, including experience. Pittsburgh had won the title just two years earlier. Rodgers, who sat for three seasons behind Favre before moving into the starting lineup, was in his initial Super Bowl; Pittsburgh's Ben Roethlisberger was in his third, winning the previous two.

To perhaps even out that disparity, Rodgers consulted Steve Young, who took San Francisco to the 1995 Super Bowl win. "I wanted to talk to a lot of guys who'd been there and had success in the NFL," Rodgers said. "Steve obviously had a very similar [situation], being a guy who followed a legend [Joe Montana]. Steve has been a great guy to lean on and he's made time for me and is somebody who I really appreciate."

For Packers Nation to truly and fully appreciate Rodgers, though, he'd need to emulate Bart Starr and Favre and deliver a championship. He was more than equal to the task.

Rodgers threw for three touchdowns, two to Greg Jennings, as the Packers built an early lead and held on to win 31–25. Perhaps most significant was a clean sheet: Rodgers was not intercepted, didn't force passes under pressure (he was sacked three times), and outplayed Roethlisberger, who was picked twice.

That his 304 yards in the air and overall helmsmanship would earn Rodgers MVP honors seemed a given. That he'd finally sent Favre's massive shadow scurrying into retirement, too, was nearly as noteworthy to Cheeseheads everywhere, if not to the quarterback himself.

"I've never felt like there's been a monkey on my back. The organization stood behind me, believed in me," said Rodgers, who slipped to No. 24 in the 2005 draft before general manager Ted Thompson grabbed him. "I told Ted back in 2005 he wouldn't be sorry with this pick. I told him in '08 that I was going to repay their trust and get us this opportunity."

Opportunity seized. Comparisons dropped.

"Aaron is Aaron. Aaron and Brett are two totally different quarterbacks," Jennings said. "Aaron brings a lot of great things to the table. Obviously, Brett—he set his own legacy. He laid down his own legacy. I say, let Aaron form his own legacy and let him be Aaron."

Super Bowl XLVI

OTHER THAN PEYTON MANNING LEADING HIS TEAM THERE HIMSELF, what could seem more natural for the first Super Bowl hosted by Indianapolis than for younger brother Eli to take the Giants that far?

And who else but Peyton's biggest NFL rival, Tom Brady, to be on the other sideline at Lucas Oil Stadium for the 2012 edition?

While Peyton sat out the entire season because of neck surgeries—he would be released soon after Super Bowl XLVI by the Colts and land in Denver—the family tradition was carried on by Eli. Yes, Eli was considered the lesser of the two quarterbacks, not close to a cinch Hall of Famer like his sibling. Eli wasn't even the central figure at the position in this matchup, with the spotlight shining brightest on Brady—another sure Hall of Famer.

Still, Indy could be Eli's town on this special occasion. It could be payback for those times years before when Peyton treated him like, well, a kid brother.

As he had done throughout the 2011 season while recovering, Peyton tried to keep a low profile during Super Bowl week. Had the game been anywhere but Indy—Peyton's Place—he might have succeeded.

Instead, there was as much focus on whether Peyton would return to the NFL, and where, as there was on his brother and his top rival.

"When you get to a Super Bowl, even though it's the second [recent] one for the Giants, you want the focus to be on that achievement," said Tony Dungy, who coached Peyton to that 2006 NFL championship. "Peyton would much rather have the focus on Eli and what they've done to get here, and unfortunately, that's not going to happen."

Asked if that bothered him, Eli shrugged.

Mario Manningham

Not nearly the unlikely star that former teammate David Tyree was four years earlier, Mario Manningham at least had a resume of success before grabbing the spotlight.

And we do mean grabbing it.

Manningham came out of Michigan in 2008 as a third-round draft pick who averaged nearly 17 yards a reception for the Wolverines, scoring 27 touchdowns in three seasons. The Giants saw him as a potential successor to another Michigan wideout who had done them proud, Amani Toomer, a key to New York's 2007 league title.

Manningham never reached the level of Toomer, the Giants' career receptions leader. He never really became Eli Manning's primary target.

Except in this Super Bowl, in the most critical spot.

Trailing the Patriots 17–15 late in the fourth quarter, the Giants were pinned at their 12 yard line. New England knew New York had little choice but to throw, so the Patriots concentrated mainly on Hakeem Nicks, Manning's No. 1 receiver who would finish with a game-high 10 receptions for 109 yards.

Second in New England's thoughts was Victor Cruz, the dangerous slot receiver.

Manningham? Well, yeah, the Patriots had to cover him, too, but he probably wasn't a big threat.

Yet when Manning dropped back on first down he looked left and let fly. A streaking Manningham, covered by not one but two

"When I talk to Peyton, he does a great job of trying to keep me relaxed," Eli said in his 'Aw, shucks' manner. "[We] talk a little football and talk about New England some. He's supported me this week. I know he's just working hard trying to get healthy and I'm going to support him on that."

No one was asking Eli if the protracted Peyton plot bothered him after he engineered the 21–17 victory over New England in the Super Bowl, earning not only his second game MVP award, but one more championship ring than his brother owned.

Patriots who seemed to sniff out the play call, reached out with both arms and hauled in the ball over his shoulder. Then, somehow, he sneaked both feet in bounds for a 38-yard completion.

New England safeties Patrick Chung and Sterling Moore were beaten on the play, with Manningham making the catch directly in front of Patriots coach Bill Belichick. Out came the red challenge flag.

Manningham had no doubt it was a catch and that he stayed in bounds.

"It was a great ball," he said with a wide smile. "I knew where I was on the sideline. I knew I didn't have that much room and it's a good thing I wear [size] 11s because if I wore 11½s, I would not have been in."

Coach Tom Coughlin seemed a bit stunned that, yet again, one of his non-star wideouts had done the improbable.

"I think they are both spectacular catches," he said when asked to compare Tyree's to Manningham's. "I think with Mario's . . . the way he kept his feet in bounds and held on to the ball going out of bounds was a remarkable thing."

The remarkable almost made the rest of the drive seem routine. New York inexorably moved 88 yards, with two more receptions by Manningham. The Giants scored on Ahmad Bradshaw's 6-yard TD that the Patriots did not contest, figuring their only chance to not lose on a last-second field goal was to yield the touchdown with 57 seconds remaining and get the ball back.

But the Giants held on, just like Manningham on his game-changing catch.

Eli never flinched early as he set a Super Bowl record by completing his first nine passes and New York built a 9–0 lead. He didn't cower in the third quarter when the Patriots took a 17–9 edge. And he certainly didn't falter in the fourth period, leading the Giants on a winning 88-yard drive in the dying minutes.

All the while, Peyton watched proudly as his "lil bro" went big time in Peyton's backyard.

"It just feels good to win a Super Bowl," Eli said. "It doesn't matter where you are."

Super Bowl XLVII

Joe Flacco had heard the whispers. Actually, they were a lot louder than that.

Not quite shouts, but certainly noisy enough: Flacco can't win the big one.

Heck, he couldn't even get to the big one, the Super Bowl.

Still, no quarterback had made the playoffs in each of his first five seasons or won five postseason road games. Not Peyton Manning or Tom Brady. Not Joe Montana or Brett Favre. Only Flacco.

All four of his previous trips to the playoffs had included victories, just not enough of them to get within arm's reach of the NFL title.

So when the Ravens entered the playoffs after the 2012 regular season, there were mostly shrugs among NFL folks. You know, "Oh, them again. OK, which team will knock them off before the Super Bowl?"

Not Indianapolis. And, shockingly, not Denver. Although the Broncos had the AFC's best record, the Ravens pushed them to overtime with a Rocky Mountain Miracle: Flacco's 70-yard bomb to Jacoby Jones over two defenders in the dying seconds of regulation. In double overtime, Baltimore prevailed.

And not New England. If there's one team—and one quarterback— with no fear of Foxboro, it's the Ravens. And their Super Joe.

Yep, in his fifth try, Flacco made that huge step.

"He's a great quarterback," said wide receiver Anquan Boldin, who caught two touchdown passes in the Ravens' AFC championship victory. "I don't know why people keep doubting him because the bigger the situation is, the bigger he plays, and he's proven that time and time again. So maybe they'll get off his back now."

Maybe not. At least not until he carried his team to the ultimate prize.

Early on against NFC champ San Francisco, the Ravens and Flacco made the Super Bowl look like a big easy in the Big Easy. Flacco threw for three touchdowns in the first half and Baltimore built a 21–6 lead.

And when Jones sped a record 108 yards with the second-half kickoff, well, turn out the lights.

So somebody did.

Literally.

A portion of the Louisiana Superdome went dark moments later. Among those accused were:

Beyoncé, whose halftime show supposedly drained the building of its power. But the singer's set was electrified by a separate source.

The Saints, who allegedly were getting even with commissioner Roger Goodell for the bounty sanctions. But the team does not control power at the stadium.

CBS, which had a stinker of a Super Bowl on its hands and needed something to spice it up. Not that the network had anything to gain from 34 minutes of players standing around or exercising to stay loose while viewers searched for something else to watch.

The New Orleans energy suppliers.

BINGO!

"A piece of equipment that is designed to monitor electrical load sensed an abnormality in the system," Entergy and SMG, the Superdome management company, said in a statement. "Once the issue was detected, the sensing equipment operated as designed and opened a breaker, causing power to be partially cut to the Superdome in order to isolate the issue."

Until the lights came back on fully powered, the NFL was not about to resume the game.

"The funny thing is the light was actually good when the lights went out," Flacco noted. "I don't know what it looked like on TV, but I think the receivers would have still been able to see the ball in all that.

"The biggest issue was with the headsets. I think our headsets were working; I think theirs weren't."

Ray Lewis

Ray Lewis stood before his teammates and asked them for "one more ride."

In some ways, they took him on the ride of a lifetime.

The brilliant linebacker already owned a Super Bowl ring as the anchor of the devastating defense Baltimore rode to the 2000 NFL season title. As the 2012 schedule drew to an end, Lewis decided it was time.

Time to walk away from the Ravens and football.

But first . . .

"I thought we were getting our 'Let's go on a run in the playoffs' speech,'" teammate Terrell Suggs said of Lewis bringing the Ravens together for an announcement. "Not that.

"It caught me by surprise, because we all thought the great Ray Lewis was going to play forever. I thought he was going to surpass Brett Favre and still be out there doing it well into his 40s. He let us know that the sun is setting on his career. It's amazing and it's sad, all at the same time."

A month later, it was still amazing—and not at all sad.

Many great players don't recognize the slippage that comes with age, wear, and tear. Favre was like that, for sure.

But Lewis accurately read the signs at the end of his 17th pro season: a step or two slower, a bit hesitant in spots, even some time spent on the sideline. The aggressiveness didn't waver; the killer instinct remained.

Still, Lewis was not the same player and he knew it. So he simply wanted one more fulfilling achievement to go with his MVP honors for the 2001 romp past the Giants and his two Defensive Player of the Year awards (2000, 2003).

"I'll make this last run with this team, and I'll give them everything I've got," he said just before the Ravens began the playoffs against Indianapolis. "When it ends, it ends. But I didn't come back for it to end in the first round."

It didn't. Nor in the second, an upset win at Denver. Nor in the third, when the Ravens manhandled New England. Lewis had a team-high 44 tackles in that surge to the big game.

The final stop on the farewell tour was New Orleans, against San Francisco. It was the first Super Bowl in which coaching brothers, Baltimore's John Harbaugh and younger sibling Jim, faced off, a juicy storyline.

But Lewis being Lewis, the spicier plot followed him. Ever hear of deer antler spray?

Hardly anyone paying attention during Super Bowl week had—until a report surfaced that Lewis purchased the product from a company in Alabama to help him recover from a triceps injury. Deer antler spray supposedly contained a naturally occurring substance that was on the NFL's banned list.

There was nothing to the mini-controversy, but it rekindled questions about Lewis's character. A dozen years earlier, remember, he'd been accused of covering up a double slaying in Atlanta the night after the 2000 Super Bowl.

All Lewis could do, he said, was "play like Ray Lewis plays."

And while he was not a dominant force in the Super Bowl, making seven tackles but also being unable to stop several 49ers on passes or runs, he did just enough. So did the Ravens, who stopped the 49ers on three plays from the 5 yard line in the final moments and held on for a 34–31 victory.

When it was over—the game and, yes, Lewis's career—he looked up at the Superdome roof as a steady shower of confetti fell.

"To me, that was one of the most amazing goal-line stands I've ever been a part of in my career," Lewis said. "What better way to do it than on the Super Bowl stage?"

While Lewis was being lauded and applauded, an admirer with Hall of Fame residence—something Lewis will soon own—seemed choked up by it all.

"I'm jealous," Marshall Faulk said. "Ask any player, 'How do you want to end your career?' You want to tell your team, 'This is it.' You want to play in a Super Bowl and have a chance to win it. Very few guys get to leave the game with a storybook ending."

Ray Lewis did.

When play resumed, everything was working for the Niners and virtually nothing for the Ravens.

San Francisco scored 17 straight points before Flacco and the Ravens got back on track, albeit only for a short field goal by Justin Tucker when they couldn't get into the end zone from close range. When Colin Kaepernick set a Super Bowl mark with the longest TD run by a quarterback, 15 yards, it was 31–29; the two-point conversion failed.

Nearly 10 minutes remained. Time for Flacco to restore the power in Baltimore's attack.

"The one thing you can't do is get down on yourselves," Flacco said. "We were still ahead and we never lost any confidence in what we could do."

What they did was march 10 plays to another Tucker field goal.

Then they turned it over to the Ravens' defense, which didn't appear up to the challenge until San Francisco got to the Baltimore 5. That's when star linebacker Ray Lewis and his buddies got stingy, forcing three straight incompletions by Kaepernick.

The fourth-down pass to Michael Crabtree easily could have drawn an interference call on cornerback Jimmy Smith, but no flags flew.

"The final series of Ray Lewis' career was a goal-line stand," said coach John Harbaugh as his players wildly celebrated their 34–31 win.

Best of all for Flacco, along with the shiny ring and championship pedigree, he was set to become a free agent. Of course, the Ravens ponied up to the tune of $120.6 million for six years—at the time the largest contract in NFL history.

"Joe bet on himself," Boldin said. "And Joe won."

Super Bowl XLVIII

THERE WAS SOMETHING ROTTEN IN THE BIG APPLE: THE DENVER Broncos from the very beginning of the first outdoor Super Bowl in a cold weather site.

When Manny Ramirez sent the first snap of the game over Peyton Manning's head, handing the Seahawks a safety, it was clear that only one team would be competitive in the Meadowlands. That team was not the Broncos.

With so little suspense in Seattle's 43–8 romp—the Seahawks led 22–0 at halftime and 29–0 12 seconds into the second half following Percy Harvin's 87-yard kickoff return touchdown—about the only item in question late in the game was who would earn MVP honors.

The guy who did was one of the longest shots to collect the hardware in Super Bowl history.

Malcolm Smith even was a long shot to make the Seahawks. Yes, he played for Seattle coach Pete Carroll in college at Southern Cal. But he wasn't a stud linebacker, and didn't even receive an invite to the NFL combine.

Come the draft and Smith even was an afterthought for Carroll, who selected him in the final round, the 242nd player chosen. "He didn't like it, but he had to go in the seventh round," Carroll said of Smith, who only occasionally started in the seasons before the Super Bowl. "He's proven otherwise, just like a lot of other guys in our program."

Smith proved himself as a versatile backup to a group of linebackers equal to any in football. He proved himself on special teams. He proved himself in the locker room as a dependable player on a roster filled with them.

New York, New York

Start spreading the news . . . If an outdoor Super Bowl in a cold-weather site can make it anywhere, it's New York, New York.

Well, with apologies to Old Blue Eyes—who actually would have appreciated this—it was New Jersey, Sinatra's home state, that staged the game on February 2, 2014. And this one was Roger Goodell's baby almost from the outset.

Occasionally, such NFL teams as the Giants and Jets, Redskins, Patriots, and Eagles would inquire about hosting a Super Bowl. The discussions rarely got beyond, "Why would anyone want to freeze at the game?" or something similar. Then the owners would listen to and vote for pitches from cities in Arizona and Florida, Louisiana and Texas.

They even got adventurous for the 2012 contest and held it in Indianapolis. But indoors.

Goodell had another idea as far back as 2006, when he was elected commissioner. He believed holding an outdoor Super Bowl in the Northeast would be supported not only by those owners with teams in such locales, but by a majority of the franchises who understood what a groundbreaking precedent it could set.

"Some of the greatest games in NFL history have been played in the elements, games that will never be forgotten," Goodell reasoned, mentioning the Ice Bowl in 1967: Green Bay's iconic win over Dallas at Lambeau Field before heading to Super Bowl II.

When the Giants and Jets committed to a state-of-the-art venue in the Meadowlands to open in 2010, Goodell strengthened his backing of their bid for the 2014 game.

So when the voting was held in May 2010, the result seemed predetermined. But the balloting lasted four rounds, with Tampa and Miami also bidding. South Florida fell out after two rounds, then New York prevailed.

"Under normal circumstances, we probably would have walked away with the trophy," said Sandy MacKinnon of the Tampa Bay Super Bowl bid committee. "But the NFL was interested in making history with New York City and a new stadium. I think the odds were stacked against the traditional sunshine climate."

In addition to the expected support from the cold weather contingent, such powerful owners as the Saints' Tom Benson and the Cowboys' Jerry Jones were in New York's corner. "Because it's the Giants and the Jets and New York, I can reconcile it," Jones said.

"We can have that game decided by the ways the teams could get there—in the elements."

Giants quarterback Eli Manning, who knows something about the NFL's title game, believed success was a slam dunk for New York.

"Obviously it will be cold, but that's what playing football is all about. I've been in the Super Bowl and I've been to a couple of Super Bowls and if you're not in it, the Super Bowl is an event and it's kind of a place to be. And there's no better place to be than New York City for that vibe and that atmosphere."

Two days before the big game between Denver and Seattle, Goodell began his State of the NFL news conference inside a theater at Columbus Circle by saying: "One unique aspect about the focus for this year's Super Bowl has been on the weather. Of course, we cannot control the weather. I told you we were going to embrace the weather. Here we go."

With that, flakes of artificial snow fell from the ceiling above the stage, drawing laughter.

The average temperature for February 2 in the New York area historically was around the freezing mark. Real snow? Possible.

But, to the league's way of thinking, definitely worth the risk.

"I think this is obviously innovative and it's something new, but it's also unique because it's New York," Goodell added. "This is a stage, we have two teams here. Every city can't host a Super Bowl just because of the sheer enormity of this event. And it's not just a football game. We have a week full of events, we probably have well over 150,000 coming in to the New York region for this event."

As columnist Jim Litke wrote for The Associated Press: "A 180-foot-tall toboggan slide will be plopped down in Times Square, and a stretch of Broadway from 34th Street to 48th will be closed to traffic, renamed 'Super Bowl Boulevard,' and converted into a rollicking theme park, merchandise shop and concert venue called the 'NFL Experience.'"

And guess what—it worked.

The economic impact, a figure difficult to determine in such a megalopolis, probably exceeded $300 million. Although the game was a romp for the Seahawks from the very beginning, the mood was festive and the venue was, well, super.

As for the weather, try this: temperatures in the 50s at kickoff, no sign of precipitation.

Goodell, who sat in the MetLife Stadium stands, didn't even need gloves.

"I'm just fortunate to be a part of it, fortunate to get opportunities," said Smith, who had only two career interceptions before his pick and 69-yard TD run against Manning in the Super Bowl. "I'm happy to be amongst a bunch of guys that play with attitudes and chips on their shoulders. I'm happy to represent that.

"You might have been overlooked. You might feel like you can make plays and never got the opportunity. I got that opportunity."

His chances in 2013 came because of suspensions (Bruce Irvin's four-gamer) and injuries (Bobby Wagner's two-gamer). He seized them, lifting him into the rotation, placing Smith in the toughest spots in the toughest games.

Against San Francisco in the NFC title showdown, it was Smith who hauled in Richard Sherman's deflection in the dying seconds for a clinching interception.

And in the Super Bowl, Smith made 10 tackles, recovered a fumble, and his interception TD was typical of how this atypical Super Bowl went.

Atypical because it was the first true rout in a dozen years.

Atypical because it was played outdoors in the Northeast.

Atypical because temperatures in the 50s made the Meadowlands downright balmy; it was the warmest day of the year until that point.

Mostly, it was unusual because the expected cast of candidates for Super Bowl hero was outdone by an outlier. That thrilled fellow linebacker K. J. Wright no end.

"He's one of the guys that plays with a chip on his shoulder," Wright said. "He almost didn't get drafted. For him to come in, start from the bottom and work his way up to Super Bowl MVP, it shows how much character he has, how resilient he is."

That resilience was tested the next season, when Smith's playing time was severely cut. Seattle simply was too talented at his position for Smith to build very much momentum off his memorable night in MetLife Stadium.

Even so, the Seahawks got back to the big game, nearly winning it.

Regardless of where he might wind up in the NFL, Smith would always have a place with Ray Lewis and Chuck Howley as linebackers to earn the MVP accolade in a Super Bowl. His performance brought him back to the days as a child when he was counted on to get into the end zone.

"I've always just been taught to run to the ball and good things will happen for me," Smith said. "I played running back as a kid, so it's always been the most exciting thing to have the ball in my hands."

And then being able to finish off the play of a lifetime with a dunk over the end zone crossbar.

Super Bowl XLIX

AT AGE 37, TOM BRADY UNDERSTOOD HE WAS CLOSER TO THE END OF his magnificent NFL career than to the stunning beginning. He also recognized that after winning three Super Bowls before he turned 28, he'd earned none since.

So when Brady suggested before the 2014 season that he hoped to play well into his 40s, it was accompanied by assumptions he would only carry on so long as his New England Patriots were a contender.

Forget contender. Thanks to Brady's brilliance, the Patriots were champions again.

And unlike most aging veterans, Brady could relish his football future, not dread it.

"No. I've got a lot of football left," the 37-year-old said following his third Most Valuable Player performance and a historic Super Bowl rally in the 28–24 victory over Seattle. "It's hard to play this game and it takes a big commitment, a lot of sacrifice.

"It's a big challenge and it's incredible to experience this feeling once, and I've been fortunate to play on four really great teams, so I'm really blessed."

Really talented, too. Brady moved into an elite class peopled only by his boyhood idol, Joe Montana, as a three-time MVP in the big game.

This one offered quite the redemption for Brady, as if a surefire Hall of Fame quarterback would need anything of the kind. Yet after those two close-call failures against the Giants in 2008 and '12, critics had claimed Brady no longer could be counted on to make the key plays.

They pointed to his struggles against superior pass rushes and a penchant for forcing passes when heavily pressured.

As if every passer isn't plagued by exactly that.

Brady's 2015 answer: an unprecedented Super Bowl comeback against the best defense in the league.

"You know when you are going up against a Tom Brady, no lead is safe," Seahawks coach Pete Carroll said. "The guy has done it so many times, made all those plays in his career that you kind of expect he can do it again and again."

Brady already had tied Montana's mark with 11 Super Bowl TD passes, hitting Brandon LaFell and Rob Gronkowski in the first half. But Seattle owned the third period for a 24–14 lead, and no team had overcome as much as a 10-point deficit in the final quarter to win a Super Bowl.

As Seahawks fans began contemplating celebrations of their team becoming the first back-to-back champions since New England a decade earlier, Brady had other thoughts.

He put those thoughts into action—against the Legion of Boom secondary that hardly anyone had successfully challenged since it was formed in 2012.

Sticking to quick throws to keep the Seahawks' defense off-balance, Brady crisply guided New England 68 yards in nine plays—two of which were long third downs: to Julian Edelman for 21 yards on third-and-14, then again to Edelman for 21 on third-and-8. His favorite wideout turned short completions into mammoth conversions.

Then it was a 4-yard TD pass to Danny Amendola, punctuated by a fiery arm pump, to break Montana's record. More importantly, to Brady, it got New England within 24–21.

But it wasn't enough. Not yet.

When New England's defense forced a punt with plenty of time remaining, the overwhelmingly pro-Seahawks crowd at University of Phoenix Stadium sensed the ultimate confrontation was ahead. The decisive question: Could Brady lower the Boom?

"Before the drive started, Tom came into the huddle and just told us that we needed a championship drive," said halfback Shane Vereen, who had 11 receptions for 64 yards in the game, with five touches on the decisive drive. "He led us down the field and found the open receivers."

Malcolm Butler

Tom Brady as a Super Bowl savior makes sense. Malcolm Butler? Not even Butler could envision his taking that role.

Yet the undrafted rookie from West Alabama—no, not the Crimson Tide, but the Division II Tigers—made perhaps the most critical interception in the half-century of Super Bowls.

How did the backup to a backup cornerback even get on the field, let alone in position to pick off Russell Wilson's 1-yard pass at the goal line in the dying seconds?

Through hard work, determination, football smarts, and, well, a little bit of luck.

Butler wasn't even signed by a team after the 2014 draft, and only was recognized by the Patriots after attending a tryout. "We were already finished with the draft, we had signed our rookie free agents," coach Bill Belichick said. "He was part of what we like to call the few, the proud and the free that came in. He did a great job in that rookie minicamp and we kind of created a roster spot."

Then Butler created playing time by continually annoying Brady in practice; he had this nasty habit of being in position to knock down or intercept the star quarterback's throws.

Still, he was buried on the depth chart for much of 2014, making it onto the field on defense in only three games. Come the big game, though, and when veteran Kyle Arrington struggled against another obscure player, Seattle receiver Chris Matthews, the Patriots inserted Butler. The kid made the move pay off in diamonds—the kind that go on Super Bowl rings.

The final receiver was Edelman for 3 yards and the lead.

Brady completed all eight throws on the 10-play, 64-yard march. He was in total control, seemingly toying with the normally immovable Seahawks. It was reminiscent of his last-series work in Super Bowl XXXVI against the Rams for his first ring.

"Hard to remember that far back. I'm a little bit older now," he joked when asked to compare the drives. "You just have to make the plays to

All those hours of film study, all of those scrimmages trying to prove his worth, every hit on special teams would someday turn into something good, Butler figured.

How about something great.

Butler had noticed on film that when the Seahawks went into the formation they were using at the 1 yard line in the final seconds, they often threw a quick slant rather than hand off to their Beast Mode running back, Marshawn Lynch. So he crowded the inside and when receiver Ricardo Lockette made a quick in-cut, Butler was in the way.

"I just said 'If I'm wrong, I'm wrong; they're on the 1-yard line, they're going to run it anyway,'" Butler said. "But if they pass it, I'm going to be on it."

On it? He grabbed it—and soon after was holding the Lombardi Trophy.

"Malcolm made a huge play to save our season," Brady said. "It was the perfect play at the perfect time. None of us will ever forget that play."

Certainly not Brady, who only moments before the pick could be seen shaking his head in bewilderment as the Seahawks closed in on victory.

Then the Butler did it.

"He's been doing it to me in practice all season," Brady said with a smile, "so it was nice to see him pick someone else off."

Brady showed his appreciation a few days later, giving Butler the keys to the Chevrolet truck Brady won as game MVP.

"We had a meeting and he was just like, 'Congrats on the big play,'" Butler said. 'You can get the keys to that truck.'"

win. It was great. We haven't had many games this year that have come down like this."

"Like this" included the Patriots needing Malcolm Butler's goal-line interception in the dying seconds to preserve victory.

Only a few Super Bowls have come down to the final seconds, yet all six involving Brady's Patriots did. New England won four, and Edelman explained what that meant.

"Tom's the best ever," Edelman said. "I'm a big Joe Montana fan; I love him to death. I thought he was the best and everything. He won four, he's undefeated in four, but they didn't have a salary cap back then. He had some great players around him. He had some great defenses and all that.

"Tom Brady came out here, he's been to six Super Bowls. He's won four with the salary cap. It's hard to argue against that."

But the postscript dampened Brady's supernova. He was suspended by the league for a portion of the next season for his role in the deflation of footballs for the AFC title game. While Brady insisted nothing could detract from the Patriots' fourth championship, the rest of the football world was more skeptical—wondering about the legacy of this Super Bowl hero.

Super Bowl 50

How FITTING, HOW PERFECT, HOW HOLLYWOOD THAT THE GOLDEN Super Bowl would feature a quarterback closing in on his golden years. Well, not quite, but having Peyton Manning as the face of Super Bowl 50 certainly suited the NFL.

And that Manning got there after a discouraging two months of the season in which he played poorly, then was sidelined by a foot injury, added to the intrigue. Plus, at age 39, it was generally believed that Manning was on the verge of retirement.

So the prospect of the five-time league MVP riding off into the sunset with a Lombardi Trophy strapped to his saddle—just like his boss, John Elway, did after the 1998 season, which happened to be Peyton's first in the NFL—was the stuff that movies are made of.

"He hasn't said anything to me," Denver coach Gary Kubiak said in the buildup to the big game at Santa Clara, California, against the Car-olina Panthers and their own star quarterback, 2015 NFL MVP Cam Newton. "I know he's enjoying the playoffs and enjoying this opportunity with this football team. I can't speak for him. He'll have to answer those questions. But I know it's special to have him back in the huddle leading the way and I'm just very proud of his work getting back to be in this position."

Manning had gone 1-2 in previous Super Bowls, a win over Chicago in 2007, a loss to New Orleans in 2010, and a humiliating rout at the hands of Seattle in 2013. The first two came with Indianapolis, of course, but Manning was released by the Colts after sitting out the 2011 season because of neck surgeries.

Elway and the Broncos won the bidding war—a major gamble because there was no true indication Manning would ever return to his stellar form. But anyone who doubted Peyton was played for the fool when he not only was as great as ever in a Denver uniform, but added that record fifth Most Valuable Player honor in 2013.

That began to look like a last hurrah for Manning when an assortment of injuries began diminishing his skills. His arm lost strength. His throws began to flutter. He couldn't make the quick adjustments in the pocket to avoid the pass rush. Midway through the 2015 schedule, Kubiak had the unenviable task of benching Manning for untested Brock Osweiler, who had been Manning's backup for three and a half seasons. And while Manning missed seven games recuperating from a torn plantar fascia, Osweiler performed well enough to put Denver in position to win the AFC West.

And when Peyton was healthy enough to suit up again, for the first time in his Hall of Fame–bound career, he was second string. That is, until the Broncos were struggling against weak San Diego in the season finale, a game Denver needed to secure the top seed in the conference. At halftime, Kubiak sat down Osweiler and sent number 18 onto the field.

"He's never come off the bench in his life," said Peyton's dad, Archie, a former standout quarterback himself. "But the fact he did it four weeks ago and turned the game around is probably his biggest accomplishment."

Certainly one of them. The Broncos rallied to beat San Diego 27–20 behind Manning's strong second-half performance. They earned the division title, a first-round playoff bye, and home-field advantage throughout the AFC postseason.

Over in the other conference, Carolina was finest by a big margin. Newton, the 2010 Heisman Trophy winner and top selection in the 2011 draft, had emerged as the NFL's most dangerous offensive player. Standing 6'5", weighing 245 pounds, blessed with speed and power as well as a bazooka arm, Newton led the Panthers to NFC South crowns in 2013 and '14—no team had repeated as champions of that division before Carolina did it.

But in 2015, Newton took that quantum leap from good to superb. He passed for 35 touchdowns and ran for 10 more, a record combination.

The Panthers won their first 14 games before their only slip-up against Atlanta. They finished 15-1, as Newton lived up to his "Superman" persona. He also sparked some controversy, admitting that his exuberant touchdown and victory celebrations—including some dabbing and other dance moves, too—didn't appeal to everyone. Oh yes, those celebrations sure were popular with Panthers fans, especially the children in the stands to whom he would hand footballs after scores. As for the rest of America, well, here's what Newton had to say: "I'm an African-American quarterback that scares people because they haven't seen nothing that they can compare me to. . . . I'm doing exactly what I want to do, how I want to do it and when I look in the mirror, it's me. Nobody changed me, nobody made me act this certain type of way, and I'm true to my roots. It feels great but yet, people are going to say whatever they want to say."

Sadly, this became a cause celebre when the Panthers reached the Super Bowl, beating Seattle 31–24 after leading 31–0 at halftime, then routing Arizona 49–15. Not how magnificent Newton, tight end Greg Olsen, running back Jonathan Stewart, and the entire offensive line were performing. Not how All-Pros Luke Kuechly, Thomas Davis, and Josh Norman had catapulted the defense into the upper echelon. Cam and racism became a tiresome topic.

Hall of Fame tight end Ozzie Newsome, now the general manager of the Baltimore Ravens, put the issue into perfect perspective. "I was a pretty good quarterback growing up," he told the *New York Times*, "but when it came to organized football, I knew I should become a wide receiver because from everything that I was reading, all the blacks were getting their positions changed. Now you've got some heroes that you can look at; there is someone you can emulate who is black."

Yes, in the winter of 2016—nearly three decades after Doug Williams led Washington to the Super Bowl title—the race of an NFL quarterback was a serious and overblown subject of conversation. "It's almost impossible to prove because you're never going to get someone to admit it. It's very difficult to get someone to say, 'I don't like him because he's black,'" James Rada, an associate professor of journalism at Ithaca College who has studied how black and white athletes are described in broadcast media, told *USA Today* columnist Nancy Armour. "But when the things they're critiquing fall in with preconceived stereotypes, then you do have to ask the question."

Thankfully, the focus on the other Super Bowl team's quarterback centered on anything but the color of his skin. Manning and Denver's road to Super Bowl 50 had many more potholes than did Newton and Carolina's. The Broncos struggled mightily before their defense caused a fumble that led to the winning touchdown against Pittsburgh in the divisional round. And then, in an epic 17th meeting between Manning and Tom Brady, the four-time Super Bowl champion with the Patriots, Denver's offensive performance again was sporadic. Manning did throw for two touchdowns, but the outcome again came down to the Broncos' magnificent defense. It battered Brady all game, never letting him get into a rhythm. Broncos defensive coordinator Wade Phillips, the 2015 NFL Assistant Coach of the Year (Carolina's Ron Rivera was Coach of the Year), designed a variety of schemes that, combined with the constant pressure on the quarterback, had Brady throwing before he wanted to, sometimes off-balance.

Still, when Denver could do pretty much nothing with the ball in the final quarter, New England consistently threatened. Each time, the Broncos held off the Patriots. But with 12 seconds to go, Manning on the sideline with his helmet perched on his head as he stared at the video board above, Brady's fourth-down lob was caught by double-covered Rob Gronkowski for a touchdown. Denver led 20–18, and a two-point conversion would tie it.

"One play," All-Pro linebacker Von Miller said. "We needed one more play, and we were going to make that play."

Indeed, Brady once more was under siege at the snap. His pass to a well-covered Julian Edelman over the middle was deflected to Broncos cornerback Bradley Roby.

Manning was headed back to the Super Bowl, and he whispered to Patriots coach Bill Belichick on the field after the final whistle: "Hey, listen, this might be my last rodeo. So, it sure has been a pleasure."

His brother, Eli, already a winner of two Super Bowls with the Giants, wouldn't venture a guess whether this was it for Peyton. He did acknowledge it was a consideration. "I kind of think like everybody else, where you see this as possibly being the last game," Eli Manning said. "I don't know if he knows himself, or if he's thought about it. When you get to Year 19 and kind of deal with some injuries and things going on, it'd be a good way to go out. I hope that he can win this game—and if he decides to hang it up, go out on top."

In Super Bowl 50, the D in Denver stood for Defense, just as it had in the AFC championship game against New England. Dominant Defense. Peyton Manning, a five-time MVP, didn't have to be perfect or anything close to it. Not the way the Broncos' defense was playing.

Mostly, Manning could thank Von Miller, who provided extra special service from his linebacker position in Denver's surprisingly easy 24–10 victory over Carolina.

Call it Shock and Awe, football style. Miller spearheaded the Broncos' big-play defense to win the MVP award and hold the Panthers to their fewest points all season.

Miller was in the middle of everything: two and a half sacks for 27 yards, six tackles, two forced fumbles, and two quarterback hurries. He stripped the ball twice from Carolina's All-Pro quarterback Cam Newton, the NFL's MVP during the regular season. The second strip in the fourth quarter set up the clinching touchdown for Denver.

Forget about linebacker legends such as Jack Lambert and Lawrence Taylor for the moment. Miller's performance, and that of the rest of the Denver defense, was truly one for the ages.

"I'm glad we didn't have to play against our defense," said Manning, who watched his defense make life miserable for Newton.

No, but Manning had to face the hordes of media with the same tiresome question in the days leading up to the Super Bowl: If the Broncos won, would he retire?

Naturally, his team desperately wanted to win this one for the respected quarterback. And one for themselves for a very special reason: to wipe out the bitter feelings of that crushing 43–8 loss to Seattle two years earlier. Following that rout, Broncos executive vice president John Elway decided his team needed more defense if it was going to win a Super Bowl. So he added linebacker/end DeMarcus Ware, cornerback Aqib Talib, and safety T. J. Ward. He had drafted defensive linemen

Derek Wolfe and Malik Jackson in 2012. With Miller leading the way, all those players made huge contributions to the Broncos' Super Bowl 50 win.

Newton was simply outplayed. Denver befuddled him, maybe even intimidated him a bit. "We dropped balls, we turned the ball over, gave up sacks, threw errant passes," Newton said. "That's it. They scored more points than us."

The matchup featured two distinctly different styles: Carolina as the top offensive team in football and Denver with the top defense.

"We came into the game wanting to play our defense," Miller said. "We knew if we were to be consistent and play our style of defense that we'd be able to come out on top." Denver dominated from the start.

Following a 34-yard field goal on the opening series by Brandon McManus to give the Broncos a 3–0 lead, Miller came roaring in from the left. He stripped the ball from Newton at the Carolina 5. Jackson fell on it in the end zone for a 10–0 Denver lead.

In the second quarter, Newton finally got the Panthers in gear on a 73-yard drive that ended with Jonathan Stewart leaping over the line for a 1-yard TD. The Broncos got another field goal by McManus to take a 13–7 lead at halftime—even though Manning did little to help with only 76 passing yards and one interception.

In the third period, Ted Ginn Jr. caught two passes for 45 yards to move Carolina into field goal range. At this crucial point, Denver added some luck to its repertoire. Carolina kicker Graham Gano's field goal try clanked off the top of the right upright, turning the ball back to Denver.

Then McManus kicked his third field goal of the game and 10th in as many postseason attempts, this time from 30 yards, for a 16–7 lead.

Denver's defensive schemes under coordinator Wade Phillips were giving Newton fits. The Broncos were clamping down on the perimeter and keeping Newton from running, not giving an inch. Newton found himself harassed on nearly every snap. When he was flushed out of the pocket, he was rushing throws and unable to find a rhythm.

"Their whole team was rattled once we started hitting 'em, running backs fumbling the ball, them throwing," said Broncos cornerback Chris Harris Jr. "They haven't been hit how we hit."

One quarter to go to crown a champion for the 50th time in the Super Bowl era.

With 10:26 left in regulation, Gano made up for his third quarter flub by kicking a 39-yard field goal just inside the right upright to cut Denver's lead to 16–10. The Broncos were so bogged down on offense that the Panthers kept getting the ball back quickly. So, despite generally being outplayed much of the day, Carolina remained in position to steal the victory.

Then came the deciding play of the game. Miller capped his MVP performance by once again stripping the ball from Newton on third-and-9 from the Carolina 25 with four minutes left. The ball bounced forward a couple of yards in front of Newton, who took a couple of steps toward it before backing off.

There was a major pileup as the ball lay on the ground after Miller forced the fumble. Newton looked as if he was frozen to the spot as Broncos safety T. J. Ward leapt on the ball. "We were hungry for that one. We saw that ball, and it was like hyenas on an antelope," said Ward.

Newton would be heavily criticized in the aftermath for not going all out to recover the loose ball. In football parlance, he was said to have made a "business decision." That phrase is no compliment.

That turnover set up the Broncos' only offensive touchdown. C. J. Anderson scored from 2 yards. Bennie Fowler caught the two-point conversion for the 24–10 final.

In winning the Super Bowl MVP award, Miller became the first linebacker in 34 years to get two and a half sacks and an interception in a playoff game.

"If I could cut this award, I would give it to DeMarcus [Ware] and [Derek] Wolfe and all the other guys," Miller said. "The Super Bowl MVP is special, but the Super Bowl ring is something that I will keep with me for the rest of my life."

Manning, most everyone's sentimental favorite, had struggled, at times looking old and certainly less than ordinary. He was 13 of 23 for 141 yards, threw one interception, and lost a fumble.

Oh, yes, he also won his second Super Bowl ring. The imperfect game was the perfect ending for Peyton Manning.

Super Bowl Coaching Heroes

FOR ALL THE DOZENS OF STARS WHO HAVE MADE THEIR MARKS ON THE
Super Bowl through nearly 50 years with their athletic skills—call them
the Big Game Brawn—there are the masterminds on the sidelines. Call
them the Big Game Brains.

While every head coach who ever earned a championship ring
deserves a shout-out, here's our tribute to the eight that had the most
significant impact on the NFL's grand party, the Super Bowl.

VINCE LOMBARDI, GREEN BAY

Super Bowl Titles: Two (1967, 1968)

Super Claim to Fame: Lombardi was nearing the end of his tenure in
Green Bay when he led the Packers to the first two Super Bowl
crowns. A stickler for detail, his squads in those victories against
Kansas City and Oakland were deeper, more versatile, and far better
prepared than the opponents.

Coming Through under Pressure: All of the NFL looked down on the
AFL when the merger came. Lombardi heard from every coach and
many owners in his league about how the Packers were not just representing Green Bay, but the establishment that was the NFL. They
basically told him he dare not lose.

Specialty: Passion. A taskmaster, a drill sergeant, even a dictator, Lombardi also was as fervent about performing well and winning as
anyone in the sport. It rubbed off on the players, who personified
what Lombardi meant by his most famous saying: "Winning is not a
sometime thing, it is an all the time thing. You don't do things right
once in a while . . . you do them right all the time."

Tom Landry, Dallas

Super Bowl Titles: Two (1972, 1978)

Super Claim to Fame: Landry was the first head coach to bring his team to six Super Bowls. He also brought to the game the shotgun offense that had lost favor in the NFL, and the Flex Defense, manned by the Dallas Doomsday Defense.

Coming Through under Pressure: A year after what remains one of the worst Super Bowl performances by a team and a coaching staff in a loss to an inferior Baltimore team, Landry brought the Cowboys back to the title game against Miami. It was a rout—in the Cowboys' favor—from the outset.

Specialty: Composure. Some say if there was a Mount Rushmore of NFL coaches, Landry would be on it because he seemed to be chiseled out of rock anyway. Decked out in a sport jacket and tie, with his ever-present fedora atop his head, Landry never lost his cool on the sideline. A brilliant strategist, he could examine the action and find the correct approach while others around him might be panicking.

Don Shula, Baltimore, Miami

Super Bowl Titles: Two (1973, 1974)

Super Claim to Fame: OK, we first have to note that Shula was on the wrong coaching end of the biggest upset and most significant of all Super Bowls, the 1969 loss to the Jets. But Shula also guided the Dolphins to the only undefeated, untied season in pro football history, capped by the win over Washington in Super Bowl VII.

Coming Through under Pressure: Having lost in his first two Super Bowl trips, and with no defeats on his Dolphins' resume during the 1972 season, Shula stared down the unprecedented with the '73 victory that finished off a 17-0 campaign. Not even Bill Belichick, with a more-talented group at the 2008 game, could match Shula's achievement.

Specialty: Longevity. The winningest coach in pro football history, Shula went 347-173-6, including the postseason. He coached the Colts for seven years, going 71-23-4 in the regular season. Shula was Miami's boss from 1970 to 1995, with only two losing seasons. Shula looked like a football coach, too, with a rock-hard chin that was, frankly, intimidating.

CHUCK NOLL, PITTSBURGH

Super Bowl Titles: Four (1975, 1976, 1979, 1980)

Super Claim to Fame: Noll took over a team that had never sniffed a championship and turned Steel City into Super Bowl City. Nine future Hall of Famers were drafted under his watch. And while Noll often is cited for putting together Pittsburgh's Steel Curtain, he was wise enough to know when to let the horses run free on offense, too.

Coming Through under Pressure: Noll recognized exactly what the Steelers needed to do to win. If his defense was dominating, as it so often was, he'd call an even more aggressive game for his defenders. When the Steel Curtain dropped on an opponent, there rarely was a response. And when Noll knew Pittsburgh couldn't win on D alone, he let Terry Bradshaw, Franco Harris, John Stallworth, and Lynn Swann do their thing. Which, of course, was scoring lots of points and winning.

Specialty: Motivation. That was Noll's main virtue, even as he took over a franchise that had never won a playoff game. He immediately changed the football environment in Pittsburgh, once noting that "being respectable is for losers." Never a friend with the players, he wasn't an enemy, either. He was a superb motivator who understood the need to keep his distance as an authoritative figure. But virtually everyone who played for Noll said they would run through, well, a Steel Curtain for him.

BILL WALSH, SAN FRANCISCO

Super Bowl Titles: Three (1982, 1985, 1989)

Super Claim to Fame: Considering that Walsh put together the 49ers roster that won the Super Bowl in 1990 under George Seifert after Walsh prematurely retired, he sort of has as many rings as any coach. Regardless, Walsh's teams were easy on the eyes, yet ruthlessly efficient.

Coming Through under Pressure: Two of Walsh's Super Bowl victories—the first and last—were tight affairs in which the Niners either had to protect a lead or rally, both times against Cincinnati. But the most pressurized of those championship contests was against Miami and passing sensation Dan Marino. Asked how the 49ers would slow down the record-setting Marino, Walsh half-frowned and simply said: "We have a pretty good one of those, too," referring to Joe Montana. Montana outplayed Marino, who was harried by San Francisco's defense for much of a 38–16 49ers romp.

Specialty: The West Coast Offense, still a staple of the NFL three decades later. Short drops by the quarterback. Quick, precise routes by the receivers. Perfect timing. Walsh didn't invent that type of attack; he merely refined it. He also saw in Joe Montana something every other NFL team did not, drafting Montana in the third round in 1979. Montana was exactly what Walsh's offense required.

JOE GIBBS, WASHINGTON

Super Bowl Titles: Three (1983, 1988, 1992)

Super Claim to Fame: Gibbs won Super Bowl championships with three different quarterbacks: Joe Theismann, Doug Williams, and Mark Rypien. The other head coaches on this list got their titles with the same QB.

Coming Through under Pressure: It's difficult enough to win an NFL championship in a normal year. Two of Washington's Super Bowl wins came during years interrupted by a players strike. That Gibbs could keep his team united in the 1982 and 1987 seasons, then win it all speaks to his incomparable leadership skills.

Specialty: Offense. Gibbs was an offensive maestro, combining a power running game with precise passing and a flair for the deep ball. But his most impressive work might have been done in the trenches, helping put together "The Hogs," the most Super of all offensive lines.

JIMMY JOHNSON, DALLAS

Super Bowl Titles: Two (1993, 1994). He probably would have won more had he not feuded with owner Jerry Jones and left after the second championship.

Super Claim to Fame: JJ's hair. Just kidding—though not by much. The college-trained Johnson really is the only head coach from those ranks to put together a Super Bowl championship run. He was dismissed early on as an interloper in the pros. Shame on those who underestimated Johnson.

Coming Through under Pressure: Few jobs in any sport carry more built-in angst and garner more intense scrutiny than coaching the Dallas Cowboys. Following a beloved legend in Landry made it extra difficult for Johnson. No matter—within four seasons, America's Team was back on top.

Specialty: Player selection. Johnson made more than 100 transactions in the early years when he took over from Landry, repeatedly finding players who fit his style and system. He engineered the biggest heist in NFL trading history with the Herschel Walker deal to Minnesota, through which Johnson acquired many core players who brought the Cowboys back to prominence. Johnson also was a brilliant motivator who, unlike some other coaches on this list, did not try to shackle his players' personalities. His Cowboys were a wild bunch. They also were winners.

BILL BELICHICK, NEW ENGLAND
Super Bowl Titles: Four (2002, 2004, 2005, 2015)

Super Claim to Fame: Only the second coach to win four, along with Noll, Belichick is tied with Shula for six appearances. But he's 4-2, while Shula went 2-4.

Coming Through under Pressure: New England's four Super Bowl crowns have been won by a combined 13 points. Every one of the wins—and both losses—were decided in the final minutes. Thankfully for Belichick, he has had difference makers Tom Brady at quarterback and Adam Vinatieri (early on) as his placekicker.

Specialty: Some would stay cheating, considering the "Spygate" and "Deflategate" scandals, and who knows what else that was kept quiet within the NFL's inner sanctum. But Belichick should be credited for his adaptability. His 2002 and 2004 Super Bowl winners were mostly conservative on offense, powerful and opportunistic on defense, Belichick's specialty. But as Brady progressed from raw quarterback to superstar passer, Belichick opened up the offense, making sure he found weapons to complement Brady.

Super Bowl Antiheroes

The Coaches

Dan Reeves, Bud Grant, and Marv Levy belong to an exclusive losers' Super Bowl club.

Each had the dubious distinction of coaching in four Super Bowls— and losing them all. All three were still respected, successful coaches, and two of them (Grant and Levy) are in the Pro Football Hall of Fame.

Dan Reeves

Despite the continuous disappointments, only one of Reeves's four losses left a lasting impression on him. "The loss to San Francisco really was the low point," the former Denver Broncos coach said regarding a 55–10 embarrassment to the 49ers in Super Bowl XXIV. "We never were a factor in the game."

Reeves and his Broncos made Super Bowl appearances in the 1986, '87, and '89 seasons, and then he was the coach when the Atlanta Falcons advanced to the big game in the 1998 season and lost.

His frustrations began in Super Bowl XXI when Reeves's Broncos lost 39–20 to the New York Giants to cap the 1986 season. The following year, Reeves tasted defeat again, this time 42–10 by the Washington Redskins in Super Bowl XXII. Then came the record-setting loss to the 49ers before Reeves, now coaching for Atlanta against his old team, sustained a 34–19 loss to the Denver Broncos in Super Bowl XXXIII.

Reeves had spent a major part of his coaching career in Denver, 12 years in all. The loss to the Broncos on January 31, 1999, came eight months before Reeves was selected for induction into the Colorado Sports Hall of Fame, causing him to quip: "I must have made the people in Denver happy."

In 23 seasons as a head coach in the NFL, Reeves coached the Broncos, Giants, and Falcons, finishing at 190-165-2. A former player and coach with the Dallas Cowboys, Reeves played in or coached in a record nine Super Bowls. He was most identified with his time in Denver, where he posted a 110-73-1 record for a .601 winning percentage.

"But for some reason, we never played as well in the Super Bowl as we were capable of playing," said Reeves.

Bud Grant

Once looking back on his four Super Bowl visits with the Minnesota Vikings, Grant said he didn't think the Kansas City Chiefs team that beat him in 1970 was very good. That was the era when the NFL champions (the Vikings) met the AFL winners (Kansas City Chiefs) for what was then the dawning age of the Super Bowl. There were three previous Super Bowls before the Vikings lost to the Chiefs 23–7 to leave the first four games between the leagues divided at 2-2.

Grant called Super Bowl IX against the Pittsburgh Steelers, a 16–6 defeat, "a terrible game." It was mostly a defensive game matching Pittsburgh's Steel Curtain against Minnesota's Purple People Eaters.

Grant was more complimentary toward the Vikings' next Super Bowl opponent, the Miami Dolphins. "Miami was certainly one of the best teams we played," Grant said. It was the closest the Vikings came to victory in the Super Bowl, as Grant recalled. "We fumbled on the Miami 1. We returned the second-half kickoff to the Miami 13, and they called it back. We had a third-down penalty that gave them a first down on the 4, from where they scored. Take these three plays out of the game and we could have won." As it was, the Vikings lost 24–7 to the Dolphins in Super Bowl VIII.

On Grant's next visit to the big game, the Vikings were beaten 32–14 by the Oakland Raiders in Super Bowl XI.

Marv Levy

Marv Levy, the most successful coach in Buffalo Bills history, led his team to four Super Bowls. Even more amazing: Buffalo lost all four in consecutive years, a mark that might never be matched.

Not that anyone would want to.

From the 1990 to 1993 seasons, the Bills fell to the New York Giants, the Washington Redskins, and twice to the Dallas Cowboys.

In the first Super Bowl meeting with Dallas, the Bills were crushed 52–17, plagued by an almost unfathomable nine turnovers. In the second meeting, there was hope at halftime. The Bills led 13–6. But they fell apart in the second half and victory was not to be. The final score: 30–13 for the Cowboys.

Quarterback Jim Kelly took the four straight losses in the big game, the most frustrating moments in an otherwise splendid Hall of Fame career. Levy didn't win Super Bowls, but no one would consider him a loser. He might be the only coach who will ever guide a team to four consecutive Super Bowls.

He certainly wasn't a quitter. Before the fourth Super Bowl, he told his team: "The only way I can assure you that you'll never lose a Super Bowl game is, don't get in it."

THE ASSISTANT COACHES

Being on the losing side in the Super Bowl is no fun. It's worse when you are one of the main reasons your team lost. Just ask Mike Martz, Darrell Bevell, and Bill Arnsparger.

Mike Martz

Mike Martz was known as an offensive wizard who would come up with surprising plays he seemed to have made up on the spot.

The St. Louis Rams' explosive offense was known as the "Greatest Show on Turf." But when it faced Bill Belichick's New England Patriots, it was humbled. Even though the Rams were 14-point favorites, they were embarrassed in one of the biggest upsets in Super Bowl history (XXXVI), New England's 20–17 victory.

"Mad Mike" later came up with a shocking confession: Instead of running the ball against the Patriots, he should have passed more.

"I was that far from doing it," Martz said, holding his thumb and forefinger a half-inch apart. "I just didn't have the courage to do it."

Darrell Bevell

Super Bowl XLIX became the butt of late-night jokes. People were asking, "What happened?"

The Seattle Seahawks were one yard away from winning against the New England Patriots. They had the best short-yardage running back in the league, Marshawn Lynch, to get that one yard. They had three tries to go three feet, so it was obvious that offensive coordinator Darrell Bevell would call a running play.

Not so obvious, it seems. In a stunning decision, Bevell called for a pass on the first try. Bad call.

Interception. Game lost. Championship lost.

The comedians had a field day. Twitter and social media were rampant with comments. The funny one-liners even reached the David Letterman show.

"I'm not a professional football coach, [but] you got a guy who scored 214 regular-season touchdowns," Letterman said. "I'd say, 'Hey, what about that guy?'"

Bill Arnsparger

Bill Arnsparger was a defensive genius for the San Diego Chargers. Not in Super Bowl XXIX, however.

That day, the Chargers were beaten by the San Francisco 49ers, 49–26.

They weren't just beaten; they were humiliated right from the beginning. In the first five minutes, the 49ers scored two touchdowns.

"We couldn't stop them," said Chargers cornerback Darrien Gordon.

On San Francisco's first series with the ball, Arnsparger's defense somehow had a linebacker covering Jerry Rice. Rice merely was the NFL's most dangerous receiver.

Touchdown. Game over.

The Players
Players have had their share of Super Bowl distress too.

Andre Reed: Four Great Performances, Four Losses
Reed played in four consecutive Super Bowls for the Buffalo Bills. All anyone remembers is that his Bills lost all four games, from 1991 to 1994. In those games, he made a combined total of 27 receptions and 323 yards.

"All the catches, all the yards, all the touchdowns are great," Reed said, "but there will always be a void there for not having won the Super Bowl."

Scott Norwood: Wide Right
Buffalo's Scott Norwood could have kicked himself after missing possibly the most famous Super Bowl field goal try. While onlookers held their breath, the ball went right and away from the goalposts in the final seconds. So did the chance of Super Bowl glory. The result: a 20–19 loss to the Giants in Super Bowl XXV. And the popularization of "Wide Right."

Thurman Thomas: Lost and Found
Thurman Thomas missed the first two plays of Super Bowl XXVI looking frantically for his missing helmet.

"I think it will be a great trivia question one day: Who started Super Bowl XXVI for Thurman Thomas while he was looking around for his helmet?" Thomas joked.

The answer: his backup, Kenneth Davis.

It didn't matter because the Bills were soundly defeated 37–24 by the Washington Redskins.

Jackie Smith: The Drop
You know him. He's the guy who dropped the Super Bowl pass that cost the Dallas Cowboys a critical touchdown. You've seen him wide open in the end zone in replays dozens of times around Super Bowl time. Known as "The Drop," it is a moment Jackie Smith wishes everyone would forget. He dropped a pass from Roger Staubach in the third period that would have tied the game. Pittsburgh won 35–31 in Super Bowl XIII.

Leon Lett: Premature Celebration

Everything was going great for Leon Lett in Super Bowl XXVII. His Dallas Cowboys were winning by a large margin over the Buffalo Bills.

Suddenly, the 6-foot-6, 287-pound defensive tackle picked up a fumble at the Dallas 35 yard line. The field was wide open—he was on his way to a touchdown and Super Bowl glory, his first TD since pee wee football.

Time to celebrate. But wait! Only one yard to go. So excited, Lett slowed a bit to savor the moment, held the football out to the side.

Uh oh! The ball was gone, knocked from Lett's hand at the 1 yard line by Bills wide receiver Don Beebe.

"How could I hear someone that small and that fast," Lett said. "I was the one making all the noise."

No touchdown. No glory. Only a touchback, and Buffalo took over.

Neil O'Donnell: Two for the Show

Except for two interceptions by the Dallas Cowboys, quarterback Neil O'Donnell performed heroically for the Pittsburgh Steelers in Super Bowl XXX.

But O'Donnell's two interceptions cost the Steelers the game. So what will everyone remember? O'Donnell bringing back the Steelers from a two-touchdown deficit, or O'Donnell's two picks? The latter, of course.

O'Donnell's first errant throw was picked off by Dallas cornerback Larry Brown. "The first one just slipped totally out of my hands," said O'Donnell.

Losing 13–0, O'Donnell led the Steelers back. Now they trailed 20–17 with 6:36 to go.

Soon, it was the Steelers' ball in the closing minutes, a three-point game. Now came the final drive from the Steelers 32.

But another interception by Brown—the result of miscommunication, according to the players—ended the Steelers' drive for "One for the Thumb."

The Cowboys cashed in their chances and held on for a 27–17 victory.

Fran Tarkenton: The Scrambler

Fran Tarkenton was nicknamed "The Mad Scrambler" for his ability to run around the backfield to avoid being sacked. Tarkenton led the Minnesota Vikings to the Super Bowl three times in the 1970s. Unfortunately for Tarkenton, he lost all three.

"I've not forgotten. Every day and every night, it pisses me off," Tarkenton once told *Vikings Now*.

Though Tarkenton is a Hall of Famer, he believes the zero in the win column keeps him from being considered among the best quarterbacks ever.

"They will never mention me," Tarkenton said. "That's fine. Because we never won a Super Bowl."

Dan Marino: Only One Chance

Dan Marino made a reputation as the quarterback with the quickest release and one of the strongest arms in the game. One of the greatest quarterbacks of all time, Marino did just about everything for the Miami Dolphins from 1983 to 1999. The one thing he couldn't do was win a Super Bowl. In fact, he only got to one, falling to San Francisco in Super Bowl XIX. He still feels a void in his career, as Marino told NBC Sports.

"When I'm watching the Super Bowl, that's going to be coming into my mind for sure. That's just part of life, man. I never had that feeling, and that's the feeling you want to have as a player as you've worked your whole life."

Three Breaking Bad: Eugene Robinson, Stanley Wilson, and Barret Robbins

At Super Bowl XXXIII, Atlanta Falcons free safety Eugene Robinson was looking for action. It had nothing to do with football.

While his teammates slept soundly in their Miami hotel, Robinson was prowling an area known for prostitution and drugs. Unfortunately, he found what he was looking for.

Robinson walked right into a police sting operation. He was promptly arrested and charged with soliciting an undercover female police officer for oral sex.

File it under Players in Major Trouble at the Super Bowl. Not only Eugene Robinson. Think about how Stanley Wilson and Barret Robbins felt after their problems cast them in a devastating, headline-making light.

The day before the 2003 Super Bowl, Robbins disappeared after going on a binge in Tijuana. In 1989, Wilson was found in a drug-induced state in a hotel room the night before the Super Bowl game.

Robinson fared better—he got to play. After he was released by authorities, Robinson went directly to Falcons coach Dan Reeves. The coach gave Robinson the option to play or sit out the game. Robinson decided to play; he did not play very well. He missed at least three tackles in the first half and got beaten on a long touchdown pass in the second quarter. The Falcons were routed, 34–19, by the Denver Broncos.

Wilson, meanwhile, missed his chance to play in the Super Bowl when officials found him the night before in a cocaine stupor in his hotel room. His Cincinnati Bengals lost 20–16 to the San Francisco 49ers in Super Bowl XXIII.

Wilson had a relapse of earlier drug problems. It was the beginning of the end of a promising career for the University of Oklahoma running back who was later sent to jail for burglary.

Robbins, an All-Pro center with the Oakland Raiders, spent Super Bowl Sunday in a San Diego hospital after disappearing from the team's hotel the night before. He had been on a drinking and drug binge on the eve of Super Bowl XXXVII.

Robbins, a 6-foot-3, 320-pound lineman, reportedly had stopped taking his medicine for depression. He had missed a team meeting, a position meeting, and a walk-through practice Saturday on the eve of the game.

Robbins was sent home by Raiders coach Bill Callahan. The Raiders lost 48–21 to the Tampa Bay Buccaneers. Callahan refused to say that Robbins's absence had any impact on deciding the game.

Robbins made a belated comeback try for the Raiders before spending several years in jail or in rehab facilities.

Sadly, the Super Bowl sometimes produced these kinds of antiheroes to go with the championship elite.

INDEX